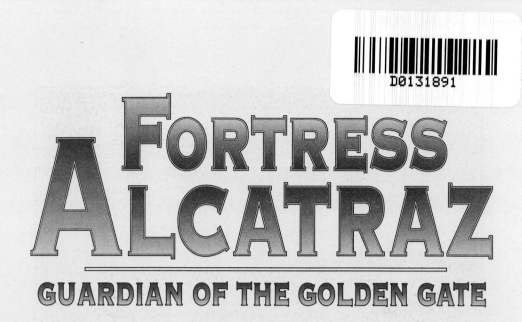

FORTRESS ALCATRAZ

GUARDIAN OF THE GOLDEN GATE

JOHN ARTURO MARTINI

TEN SPEED PRESS

Berkeley | Toronto

Copyright © 1990, 2004 by **John Arturo Martini**

Ten Speed Press
P.O. Box 7123
Berkeley, CA 94707
www.tenspeed.com

Distributed in Australia by Simon and Shuster Australia, in Canada by Ten Speed Press Canada, in New Zealand by Southern Publishers Group, in South Africa by Real Books, and in the United Kingdom and Europe by Airlift Book Company.

Previous edition published in 1991 as "Fortress Alcatraz" (ISBN 0-9629227-0-6) by **Pacific Monograph**, Kailua, Hawaii. This edition has been updated, reedited and newly designed by Pacific Monograph for Ten Speed Press.

Library of Congress in Publication Data:
Martini, John A., 1951—
Fortress Alcatraz, Guardian of the Golden Gate / John A. Martini
p. cm
Includes bibliographical references and index
ISBN: 1-58008-626-8
1. Fortification — California — Alcatraz Island — History
2. Alcatraz Island (Calif.) — History
3. Military Prison at Alcatraz Island — History
4. United States Penitenitary, Alcatraz Island, California — History
I Title
F868.S156M28 1991
979.4'61 — dc20
91-61127 CIP

Printed in the United States of America
First printing, this edition, 2004

1 2 3 4 5 6 7 8 9 10 — 09 08 07 06 05 04

CONTENTS

PROLOGUE FOOTPRINT IN THE BAY 6

1 DISCOVERY AND CONTROVERSY 8

2 THE UNITED STATES TAKES OVER 14

3 GOLD FEVER AND FORTRESS CONSTRUCTION 18

4 THE POST ON ALCATRACES ISLAND 34

5 HELIOS AND THE ISLAND FORTRESS 54

6 REBUILDING THE ISLAND 60

7 THE ROCK 72

8 CHANGING DUTY 88

9 PRISON 102

10 DISCIPLINARY BARRACKS 108

11 THE ARMY RETURN 126

12 "NO GOOD FOR NOBODY" 138

13 ABOUT THIS BOOK 144

APPENDICES 148

WALKING TOUR 152

INDEX 158

BIBLIOGRAPHY 160

FOOTPRINT
IN THE BAY

The young lieutenant of engineers leaned over his sketch of the little island. It was an oddly shaped piece of land, vaguely resembling a deformed footprint. Slightly more than 22 acres in size, the sole residents seemed to be screaming sea birds.

He made a notation above the topographical map he was preparing: *"This Island is chiefly composed of irregularly stratified sandstone covered with a thin coating of guano."* In fact, nearly the entire surface had been smeared with the droppings of uncounted generations of birds who had roosted on the island for thousands of years. The smell was overpowering.

The lieutenant and his assistant had spent several windy days scrabbling over the crumbling cliffs of the barren island. The spring winds had blown clouds of grit and sand in their faces, and swarms of enraged gulls had hindered their efforts with the surveyors' tools; chain and transit. The island, it seemed, was a major breeding area, and scores of nests dotted barren slopes.

The engineer had not been impressed by what he saw: *"The stone is full of seams in all directions which render it unfit for any building purposes & probably difficult to quarry."*

There were other, more attractive islands in San Francisco Bay. Nearby lay Wood (or Angel) Island, more than a thousand acres in size, with plenty of fresh water and thick with oak trees for firewood. Yerba Buena Island (later known as Goat Island) was the most promising prospect of all, enjoying balmy weather and with a commanding view of the only "city" on the entire Bay — a hamlet of 300 people, recently renamed San Francisco.

He concluded: *"The island has no beach & but two or three points where small boats can land."*

Lt. William Warner, U.S. Topographical Engineer and West Point Class of 1835, completed his "Field Map of Isla de los Alcatrazes" in May 1847 — more than a year before California joined the United States. Legally, San Francisco Bay and the tiny bird-covered island were still part of the Republic of Mexico.

The United States Army was already interested in Alcatraz.

American forces had seized California in 1846, and surveys of the new territory were being carried out in earnest. The military promptly realized that it was not climate or natural resources that made this little island special — it was the commanding location.

Sitting smack in the throat of San Francisco Bay, cannon on the island could sweep the inner harbor and the rivers that led into the heart of California. Alcatraz was the cork in the bottleneck of the Golden Gate.

It was also an excellent place to incarcerate prisoners.

For more than 80 years the Army of the United States controlled Alcatraz Island. In the midst of gold-rush madness, work crews arrived in 1853 and began transforming the island into an "impregnable" fortress. When the post was first occupied by troops in 1859, it was the first permanent harbor fortification on the West Coast.

During the Civil War, the island was home to 300 artillerymen who waited for an enemy that never came. They were soon joined by miscreant soldiers from other western army posts, as well as suspected Confederates from San Francisco. They were all tossed into the dungeon of the guardhouse.

After the war, Alcatraz awkwardly took on the dual duties of harbor defense fortress and ever-expanding army prison. For 20 years convict laborers worked at tearing down obsolete fortifications and re-shaping the island during a defense program that would never be completed.

Shortly after the turn of the century, the fort was officially turned into a "Disciplinary Barracks." Army prisoners constructed the world's largest and most modern concrete cellhouse atop the island — and then became its first occupants.

In 1934 the Department of Justice acquired the prison and transformed it into "United States Penitentiary, Alcatraz." The first 32 convicts were Army soldiers marooned when the military vacated the island.

During World War II the army returned, and young Coast Artillery GIs manned anti-aircraft guns on prison rooftops when they weren't pursuing the daughters of the guards.

And, in the beginning, it had been soldiers of the U.S. Army who nicknamed Alcatraz "The Rock."

Lt. Warner's original field map. This 1847 survey is the first detailed record of Alcatraz' original features. Drastic changes would occur only six years later.

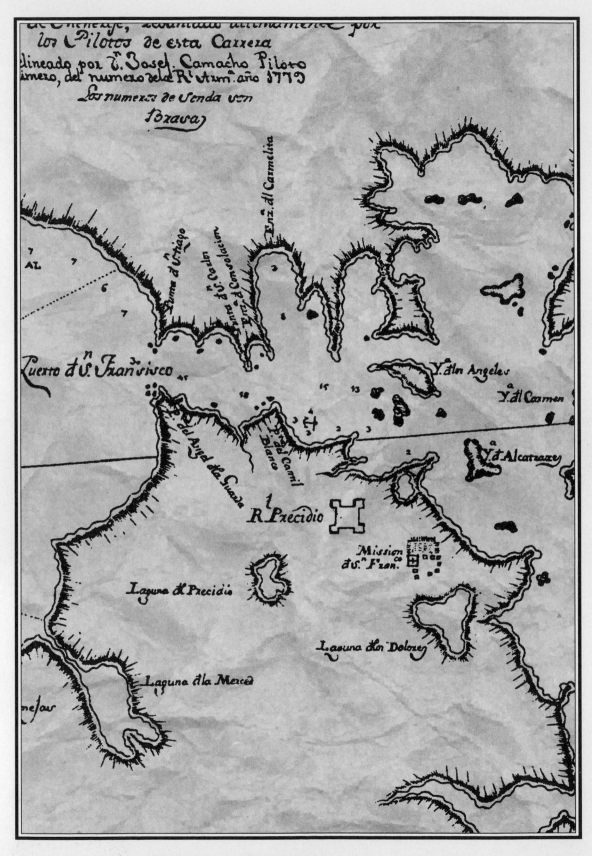

DISCOVERY *AND* CONTROVERSY

The first recorded sighting of Alcatraz Island was in 1769. A small party of Spanish soldiers, searching for the near-mythical port of Monterey, overshot their mark and stumbled across San Francisco Bay.

Spain had claimed the land known as Alta California since 1542, when Juan Rodriguez Cabrillo sailed up the coast, thoughtfully claiming all the territory he passed for his king. Cabrillo made only a few landfalls, notably at San Diego and Monterey, and rarely explored the interior of the new world he had "conquered."

What little he and following explorers saw failed to arouse the passions of the Conquistadors, and for the next two centuries the Spaniards busied themselves with subduing and exploiting the Indian empires of Mexico, Central and South America.

In the late 18th century, however, British and Russian traders began to appear on the western shores of North America. Searching for another source of wealth — otter pelts and seal furs — these foreigners threatened the Spanish Empire's long-neglected claim to Alta California.

In 1769 a land party under the command of Capt. Gaspar de Portola was dispatched from Baja California. Their orders were to proceed northward up the California coast to Monterey Bay (which had achieved near legendary status in the intervening years) and establish a site for a future military outpost and civilian settlement.

But no one had visited Monterey since 1603, and Portola's men failed to recognize Monterey Bay from 160-year-old naval charts and descriptions. Passing by Monterey Bay without realizing it, the Spaniards continued their trek up the California coast.

It was by sheer accident that one November morning Sgt. Jose Ortega found himself standing on a coastal promontory, staring at a roaring harbor opening leading to "a vast arm of the sea extending into the land."

The expanse of the harbor was overwhelming; its waters vanished into the mists of the horizon. The expedition's chaplain wrote of "a very large and fine harbor, such that not only all the

Opposite, "Plano del Puerto de San Francisco," a Spanish map dating from 1779. It shows "Alcatrazes" in the location of modern Yerba Buena Island.

A highly romanticized sketch of San Carlos, first western ship to explore the straits of San Francisco, known later as the Golden Gate. Captained by Spanish explorer Lt. Juan Manuel de Ayala, San Carlos was actually a smaller craft and had trouble wrestling with the bay currents.

navy of our most Catholic Majesty but those of all Europe could take shelter in it." Several islands were scattered inside the narrow mouth of the harbor — the strait now known as the Golden Gate.

Obviously, even to a landlubber like Portola, this was not Monterey Bay. He had either passed through Monterey without recognizing it, or there was the unlikely possibility it still lay further up the coast. But the Spaniards had no boats to cross the mouth of the harbor. The straits were rough and wind-tossed, and though no more than a mile across, a raging current could be seen pouring between the headlands. Exploration to the north had to be postponed.

Convinced that he had failed his primary mission, and concerned his men might starve during the approaching winter, Portola ordered a return to San Diego. Of his unexpected discovery, the captain noted in his diary his party had "found nothing."

As soon as the soldiers returned to Mexico and began talking about a large bay far to the north, military higher-ups realized that Portola's new harbor might well overshadow Monterey Bay in importance. The government wanted more on-site explorations.

Over the next few years other Spanish parties visited the mysterious bay, this time with strict orders to carry out detailed surveys. In

1772, standing on the hills on the eastern side of the bay, Capt. Pedro Fages looked west toward the Golden Gate and made the earliest written description of Alcatraz:

"Within the estuary we saw five islands, three of them making a triangle opposite the mouth [of the harbor], with a large distance between them; and the nearest of them to the channel at the mouth [Alcatraz] must have been over a league from it."

The first recorded ship to enter San Francisco Bay was the Royal Spanish vessel *San Carlos*. On August 1, 1775, Lt. Juan Manuel de Ayala piloted his little packet on through the Golden Gate and anchored off Angel Island. Spending the next six weeks charting the bay, Ayala used his explorer's prerogative to name the various geographical features he observed.

On August 12th he approached one of the larger rocks in the harbor. "It proved so arid and steep there was not even a boat-harbor there; I named the island de los Alcatraces (Island of the Pelicans) because of their being so plentiful there." It was the island's first European name.

Ayala noted the name "Alcatraces" on the official chart he prepared, but the island he labeled on his map was clearly today's Yerba Buena Island, two miles to the east of Alcatraz. For the next fifty years Spanish charts of San Francisco Bay identified modern Yerba Buena as Alcatraces, leaving today's Alcatraz Island as one of a number of small, anonymous rocks dotting the harbor.

In 1827 a British officer, Capt. Frederick Beechey, secured permission to carry out a survey of San Francisco Bay for the Royal Navy. The chart he prepared was far superior to Ayala's map, but for reasons unclear, Beechey juggled the names of some of the bay's geographical features.

Beechey transplanted the name Alcatraces to one of the unnamed rocks inside the Golden Gate. He then cloned the name "Yerba Buena" (Good Herb) from a small cove on the tip of the San Francisco peninsula to the island Ayala had originally designated Isla de los Alcatraces. In effect, Beechey gave the two islands the names they retain today.

Beechey also took the opportunity to name another one of the anonymous rocks in the bay after his own ship, *Blossom,* and to invent a new spelling for the Island of the Pelicans — "Alcatrasses."

No one bothered to ask the local Ohlone and Miwok Indians

THE ISLAND OF MISSPELLINGS

During its relatively short history, Alcatraz has suffered a tortuous series of variations on the original name of "Alcatraces."

Beginning with Beechey's relocating the name on his 1828 map and misspelling it Alcatrasses, and despite the U. S. Coast Survey settling on "Alcatraz" as the preferred spelling in 1851, the following variations of the name appeared up through the Civil War: Alcatraces, Alcatrasses, Alcatrazes, Alcatras, Alcatrasas, Alcatrace, Alcatrose, Alcatrazas, Alcatrazos, Alcatrases, Alcatruces, Alcatraze, Alcatrus and Alcatraz.

Americans arriving in San Francisco during the gold rush gave local landmarks their own, non-Spanish names. To the '49ers, Alcatraz was known as "Bird Island" or (as an inevitable consequence) "White Island."

JOHN CHARLES FREMONT

Explorer, Army officer, first governor of California, Fremont quickly realized the strategic value of Alcatraz and did his best to seize it for his new government.

what they called the island. If they had visited Alcatraz, the Native Americans left no evidence. This gave rise to a belief that Indians considered the island a dwelling place for evil spirits, and intentionally avoided it. It is more likely that local tribes — with the plentiful resources of the entire bay at their disposal — had little use for a barren, guano-encrusted rock surrounded by dangerous currents.

Alcatraz remained technically the property of the King of Spain until 1822, when Mexico achieved independence. Although the tiny island then came under the control of the new Republic of Mexico, no one seems to have had much interest in it until 1846. In that year Julian Workman, a naturalized Mexican citizen, obtained a land grant for Alcatraz Island. The only condition imposed by Mexico's California Governor Pio Pico was that Workman establish a navigation light upon the island as soon as possible.

Workman never erected any aids to navigation on Alcatraz, but instead transferred title almost immediately to son-in-law Francis Temple. Temple, apparently, never set foot on his barren real estate.

Workman and Temple were two of a growing number of Americans who moved to California during the 1830s and '40s. Some retained their U.S. citizenship, while some converted to Catholicism and became Mexican citizens for the purpose of acquiring land grants. As time went by, tensions grew between the Spanish Californios and the newcomer Yanquis, many of whom believed in the rather unsettling American concept of Manifest Destiny.

In the mid-1840s, relations deteriorated rapidly between the United States and the Republic of Mexico. In June 1846, some of the Yanquis took the opportunity to stage their own revolution. Taking the local Mexican commandant captive, a group of Americans seized the Mexican Army barracks at Sonoma.

The men also raised a flag of their own over the plaza in Sonoma, emblazoned with a star and a crudely painted California grizzly bear. Continuing south to San Francisco Bay, the self-proclaimed "Bear Flaggers" next scaled the steep cliffs at the narrows of the harbor entrance and spiked the cannons at a long-abandoned adobe fort in the Presidio of San Francisco.

The short-lived Bear Flag Revolt ended a few weeks later with the arrival of two U.S. warships and the raising of still another flag — the Stars and Stripes — over customhouses in Monterey and San Francisco. The Bear Flaggers were informed the United States and Mexico had officially gone to war, and California was under control of the American military. Martial law was declared throughout the territory.

At this time, John Charles Fremont, U.S. Army officer and self-appointed American governor, claimed to have purchased Alcatraz from Francis Temple. Declaring himself to be acting "as the legal representative of the U.S." Fremont supposedly paid — or agreed to pay, someday — $5,000 for the island.

When the Mexican-American War ended in 1848, the United States refused to recognize both Temple's claim to ownership of Alcatraz and Fremont's petition for reimbursement for its purchase. The government's explanation was that the original owner, Julian Workman, had never erected the lighthouse required of him, and that Fremont had never been empowered to make any such land purchases for the United States of America. All private claims were null and void. As part of Mexico's formerly undistributed lands, the island was considered public land.

Alcatraz became, and forever would be, the property of the U.S. government.

A view of early San Francisco, a year before the Gold Rush turned it into the boom town on the bay. This is Yerba Buena Cove, and in the foreground is the U.S. Navy man-of-war Portsmouth, *flanked by merchant ships chartered by the War Department to send troops to California during the Mexican War.*

THE UNITED STATES TAKES OVER

Lt. John Charles Fremont of the Corps of Topographical Engineers made a number of mistakes during the early months of American occupation of California. The U.S. Government accused him of repeatedly exceeding his authority, and even of refusing to relinquish control of the territory when the properly appointed military governor arrived. In due course, the army court-martialed Fremont.

Among the many charges leveled against Fremont was that he had exceeded his authority when he supposedly purchased Alcatraz Island. During his court martial, Fremont maintained that he had merely been acting in the interests of national security. He claimed to regard Alcatraz "as the best position for Lighthouse and Fortifications in the bay of San Francisco" — as it turned out, precisely the two purposes for which the U.S. would eventually occupy the island. His explanation carried little weight with the court, and the board censured Fremont for his actions.

The United States government wasted little time in recognizing the strategic value of Alcatraz. Shortly after capturing San Francisco, the army began to carry out preliminary surveys of the bay with an eye towards constructing fortifications. It was under this program that Lt. William Warner and the Topographical Engineers first surveyed Alcatraz in 1847. The "field map" of the island that Warner prepared was one of the first detailed land surveys carried out by the United States in California, reflecting the government's concern for building defenses on the Bay.

Less than a year after these surveys were begun, a work crew erecting a sawmill discovered gold in the American River. San Francisco seemingly grew overnight from a village of 300 people to a metropolis of 35,000. California became the focal point of world attention, and the need for fortifications became of paramount importance to the army. The little-used bay was suddenly, incalculably, valuable.

In April 1849 — at the peak of the California Gold Rush — a joint Army-Navy commission met in San Francisco to make recommen-

Opposite, a magnified daguerrotype view across the boomtown of San Francisco in early 1853 — the earliest known photograph of Alcatraz — clearly shows the island's original rounded contours, as well as its strategic location.

dations for future fortifications on the Pacific Coast. It was not a simple task. The six officers of the commission were continually hampered by the near-wholesale desertion of sailors assigned to their survey party, the lure of gold being stronger than ties to military careers. In desperation, the commission sailed to Hawaii and there hired a crew from King Kamehameha III, Kauikeaouli, in order to complete their work.

The commission announced their vision of the defense of San Francisco Bay on November 1, 1850. The plan recommended using the natural geography of the harbor to best advantage, with two multi-stored masonry forts erected at the narrowest point on the Golden Gate. One fort was to be built at Lime Point on the northern Marin shore, and another at Fort Point (so-named for the crumbling Spanish battery that stood there) on the southern San Francisco shore. These two forts would theoretically be able to concentrate the fire from several hundred cannon at a point where the channel measured less than one mile wide, presenting a devastating cross-fire to an enemy vessel trying to enter the bay.

The commissioners feared that a swift ship racing on a flood tide might be able to run past this "outer line" of fortifications. "The difficulty might be obviated by having, in addition to a strong battery on each shore at the narrowest point a third battery on Alcatrazos Island which lies within the Bay ..."

As back-up to the three large forts, the commission recommended additional batteries be constructed on Point San Jose on the San Francisco shoreline, on Angel Island, and on Yerba Buena Island. These smaller fortifications would be situated to set up an intersecting fire with the guns on Alcatraz, providing protection to the inner harbor.

If all the proposed fortifications were constructed, an enemy ship would be under constant bombardment from Mile Rock outside the Golden Gate all the way past Telegraph Hill and around to Rincon Point — a distance of seven miles.

On Nov. 6, 1850, President Millard Fillmore signed an Executive Order reserving "for Public Purposes" certain lands in and around San Francisco Bay. The areas he selected included most of the large islands in the bay, large portions of the San Francisco peninsula, much of southern Marin County, and parts of modern Vallejo. Except for the latter parcel (which, together with Mare Island, was planned for a Navy Yard), all the lands he reserved were earmarked primarily for harbor defenses.

The army immediately gave highest priority to constructing the

AND THE GOVERNMENT TAKETH AWAY

The wording of President Fillmore's phrase "for Public Purposes" may seem quaint, but it was quite intentional. All land grants given by the Republic of Mexico contained a clause stipulating that any of the lands might be "resumed by the government — when needed for public purposes." Legally, no grant was valid without this phrase. Fillmore was simply assuming Mexico's original ability to reclaim land under a policy of "eminent domain" — the right of a government to take over private property when it is in the best interests of the public good.

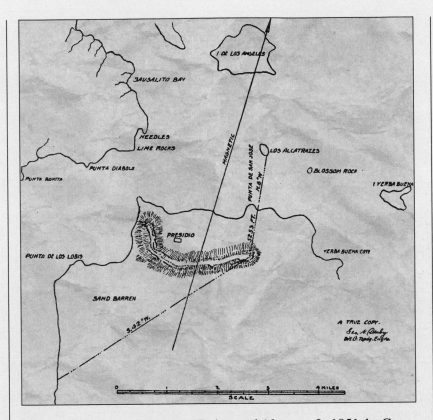

major forts at Lime Point, Fort Point, and Alcatraz. In 1851 the Corps of Engineers in Washington established a separate "Board of Engineers for the Pacific Coast" in San Francisco to design and oversee the construction of these defensive works.

In 1851 the new state of California was separated from the rest of the Union by what has been aptly described as 2,000 miles of howling wilderness. The quickest passages from the East Coast to San Francisco took six weeks, and included a land crossing of the disease-infested Isthmus of Panama. Freight delivery might take four months. Inflation was out of control.

The Board of Engineers for the Pacific Coast would be continually hampered by slow communications with the East, lack of suitable building materials, reduced budgets, soaring costs and the repeated desertion of construction workers to the gold fields.

The original estimate for constructing a fortress on Alcatraz Island was $300,000 — a figure that proved wildly conservative.

GOLD FEVER AND FORTRESS CONSTRUCTION

GOLD FEVER *AND* FORTRESS CONSTRUCTION

Construction on Alcatraz Island has always been a daunting task. Generations of soldiers, prison guards, lighthouse keepers, and park rangers can attest to that. To engineers in the early 1850s, the task must have looked insurmountable.

The uninhabited island loomed above the waters of the Bay, the tallest of two hump-like peaks reaching an elevation of 140 feet. It measured a quarter-mile long and 500 feet wide, exposed to the full force of Pacific storms funneled in through the Golden Gate. The only possible landing spot was a small cove on the eastern face. There was no way to the summit except to scramble up crumbling rock cliffs. Surrounded by swift currents and frequently obscured by fog, the island had no water, little vegetation, and minimal soil. The army had its work cut out.

Early in the summer of 1852, the engineers sat down with Lt. Warner's original topographical map and started to work out formal plans for construction of island fortifications. Their initial impression of the defensive possibilities of Alcatraz proved a bit more positive than Warner's 1847 Field Map description had led many to believe:

Opposite, the island's ordnance yard, with the original barracks building — the Citadel — in the background. The long wooden shed provided dry storage for rifled projectiles. Cannonballs, by contrast, were simply stacked in the open.

"Nature seems to have provided a redoubt for this purpose [defense] in the shape of Alcatrazes Island — situated abreast the entrance directly in the middle of the inner harbor, it covers with its fire the whole of the interior space lying between Angel Island to the North, San Francisco to the South, and the outer batteries to the West ... The walls are already mostly scarped by nature in the solid rock. A slight degree of blasting would complete this part of the work, & the battery may at once be placed at a suitable height upon the top of the Island ... The Island being high & provided with a natural scarp in many places, it has been decided to complete this escarpment [by removing the gentler slopes] so as to secure a perpendicular height of 25 feet all around ..."

The defensive works the engineers planned for the island was

The same location today — see Area #M in the Walking Tour on pages 155 and 156.

part of the "Third System" of American fortifications — the third generation of forts built by the United States. Nearly 40 forts would eventually be erected under this program on the Atlantic and Gulf Coasts. Only the two at Fort Point and Alcatraz would be built west of the Mississippi. The defenses on Alcatraz, though, would be unlike anything else the Corps of Engineers constructed.

The normal procedure for building a Third System fort was to select a location, cut the site down to sea level, and then construct a multi-tiered masonry fort with brick and stone walls as thick as fifteen feet. The engineers followed this approach at Fort Point at the narrows of the Golden Gate. Alcatraz' heights, though, were considered to be such a fine defensive feature that they decided not to tamper with the island's natural topography. At least, not at first.

The board initially recommended two batteries be constructed along the rocky bluffs. "South Battery" would be located at the tip of the island facing San Francisco and would protect the main shipping anchorage, while "North Battery" would occupy the opposite end of the island, covering the channel toward Angel Island and the passage leading to Mare Island's navy yard. The cannon in the two batteries would be mounted *en barbette* (on open platforms) in long lines girdling the cliffs.

To protect guns and crews, as well as to present a formidable obstacle to an enemy trying to scale Alcatraz' cliffs, the barbettes would be placed behind high masonry retaining walls known as scarps. From the bay, only the muzzles of the huge cannon would be visible, peering over the granite cornices of the scarp walls.

Each battery would also be provided with close-in defenses. Two-story brick towers, or *caponieres,* measuring 50 by 25 feet, would be built midway along each battery jutting out at right angles to the scarp walls. Smaller caliber cannon, firing through gun ports in the walls of these two bastions, could sweep an attacking force from the exterior faces of the scarp walls or from the gun emplacements themselves in the event the batteries were captured. Supporting the batteries and their caponierees would be an elaborate system of moats, drawbridges, soldiers' barracks and a fortified guardhouse.

In addition there were to be powder magazines, underground water cisterns, and warehouses containing enough provisions to sustain the garrison during a months-long siege.

The army entrusted the actual construction of the fortifications to the talents of a first lieutenant with the Dickensonian name of Zealous Bates Tower, West Point class of 1841. 2nd Lt. Frederick Prime, 25, three years out of the Academy, served as his assistant.

Tower arrived in San Francisco in August of 1853 and immediately made his first boat trip to Alcatraz. He was not as enthusiastic about the island as the Board of Engineers had been. He jotted down his first impressions for his superior in Washington, crusty Chief of Engineers Brig. Gen. Joseph Totten:

"The Island is rougher than I had anticipated; very rough, steep, and broken on the Eastern portion ... I have commenced the survey of the North West and South East portions of the Island. The constant prevalence of high winds delays this work much. ... The sandstone composing the Island is very friable; even where hardened on the surface it can be cut with a hatchet. Wrought iron spikes can be driven into the rock without much trouble."

Before construction could begin on fortifications, basic support facilities had to be erected. Tower and Prime constructed a temporary wharf for supplies in the sheltered cove on the island's eastern face. A compound of wooden shops, storehouses, laborers' barracks and Engineer offices was then built on the barren slope facing San Francisco above the site of the proposed South Battery.

During these first few months, the engineers ferried the laborers out to the island each day on a small sloop Lt. Tower had purchased. These construction workers, hired in San Francisco from the ranks of "busted" '49ers, were paid wages then unheard-of back East. While a trained mason might earn $2 to $3 a day in New York, his counterpart on Alcatraz was making $10 to $12. As Tower explained to his chief in Washington, "one dollar in Eastern Cities accomplishes as much as four or five dollars in San Francisco." Skilled masons were scarce and they named their own price.

The two young lieutenants soon had the men busy at work

The left flank of South Battery and its caponiere. A shortage of acceptable brick caused the engineers to build this battery from blocks of Angel Island sandstone. Atop the caponiere sits a sentry box with a crenelated roof.

blasting and cutting away at the island's slopes. Excavations initially focused on South Battery, since guns mounted there could command the entire San Francisco waterfront from the Golden Gate to Yerba Buena Island.

The engineers had chosen an elevation 40 feet above water for South Battery, and the site was laboriously terraced off to a smooth plane one-third of the way up the natural slope of the island. Sandstone foundations for the scarp walls and caponiere were then laid in concrete poured atop the natural rock of the island.

Locating suitable building materials was a problem. While some locally quarried granite was available in California, much of the rock had to be imported, some from as far away as China. To add to their supply problems, none of the locally produced brick satisfied the engineers. Most of the brick samples they tested turned out either too weak or varied widely in their dimensions.

Tower decided to try using sandstone quarried on nearby Angel Island in the construction of South Battery. Blocks of this "Blue Stone," as he described it, were set by masons in horizontal layers called "courses," then back-filled with a 15-foot thick mixture of concrete and rock rubble. Tower felt this mass of masonry was sufficient to withstand the cannon fire from any warship afloat.

The laborers simultaneously chipped roadways out of the sloping eastern face of Alcatraz to reach the site of South Battery and the future locations of North Battery and the permanent barracks. Leading from the dock to the north and south ends of the island, one branch of the road also wound its way to the highest peak by means

of a hairpin series of switchbacks. There, the Treasury Department had commenced building the first lighthouse on the Pacific Coast.

Due to the unstable rock encountered during excavations, Tower and Prime realized extensive retaining walls and revetments would be needed along the roadways and around much of the perimeter of the island. Alcatraz rock itself would proved such poor quality that the engineers only used it for crushing and mixing into concrete.

Correspondence continually passed between the lieutenant and Chief Engineer Totten as the work progressed. From Washington, Totten ordered that the proposed retaining walls should not only be more massive in size (some reaching heights of 20 feet) but that the perimeter scarp walls should also be extended above the surface of the roads at least 4 feet to give protection to troops moving along the roadways. Some "defensive walls" would also be provided with firing steps, or *banquettes,* on their reverse side for the use of riflemen during attempted landings. Even Alcatraz' roads were to be fortified.

CREATING *A* RING *OF* FIRE

As work progressed on Alcatraz, army engineers also busied themselves at Fort Point, where a conventional, three-story brick fort was under construction. Excavation of the site had been completed and initial work begun on its foundations. The Lime Point fort across the straits of the Golden Gate was being delayed, however; the landowner was demanding an exorbitant price for his property.

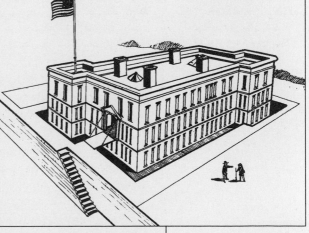

A sketch of the Alcatraz Citadel in its original configuration, surrounded by a dry moat crossed by drawbridges. Two-thirds of the structure was reserved for officers and their families, while enlisted men and laundresses occupied the remaining third.

When the Board of Engineers made the budget allocations for the 1854 Fiscal Year, a bitter rivalry arose between the supervising engineers of Fort Point and Alcatraz, each feeling that his project should receive priority. The Board eventually decided that of the $500,000 allocated to the defenses of San Francisco during the approaching fiscal year, two-thirds would go to Fort Point and one-third to Alcatraz. This unequal formula was followed for several years.

Work progressed satisfactorily on the two forts, but the War Department became concerned about the lack of existing defenses on San Francisco Bay. A war-scare with Spain over control of Cuba added to their fears.

In 1854, Alcatraz received its first armament when 11 guns were temporarily mounted on the slopes above the sites of the batteries and atop the island's two peaks. The weapons were a mixed bag of surplus navy guns and army siege cannon, and the emplacements simply "parapets (of) earth supported by barrels capped with sand bags," resembling the temporary battlefield batteries that would be erected during the Civil War. But, with no troops yet stationed on the island to fire the weapons, soldiers presumably would have rowed over from the Presidio during an attack.

Construction continued through the mid-1850s, the labor force on Alcatraz increasing to nearly 150 workers in 1857. The Board in Washington continually revised the plans for the fortifications, with such recommendations as an enlarged defensive guardhouse, additional powder magazines, and 'hot shot' furnaces for heating cannonballs.

A charming sketch of San Francisco Bay in 1857, showing laborers' barracks on the slopes above South Battery, and the Alcatraz lighthouse already in operation.

Eventually, North and South batteries were augmented by the construction of West Battery, located between the two original works and facing the Golden Gate, and by an extension to South Battery mounting four guns and named — curiously — the Three-Gun Battery. The Board of Engineers repeatedly increased the number of guns planned for these batteries. The total of proposed emplacements began as 68 in 1853, but by 1861 the number had grown to 124, with the majority of weapons sited on the western slopes of the island. The guns were to be 6-inch, 8-inch, and 10-inch caliber smoothbore cannon of the Columbiad pattern, capable of firing either solid iron shot, hollow explosive shells, or "hot-shot" cannonballs designed to set fire to wooden warships.

In addition, smaller-caliber 24-pounder howitzers were to be mounted in the two caponieres and guardhouse. These murderous weapons could spray grapeshot or canister for close-in defense.

The fort's permanent guns began to arrive in April of 1855. As the engineers had planned, the heavy Columbiads were first mounted on the barbettes of South Battery facing San Francisco. The largest of the cannon, the 10-inchers, weighed more than seven and half tons each. The workers moved the guns from dock to battery through a combination of strong backs and mule power. There were no steam engines yet available on Alcatraz to assist in the work.

The labor crews slung each weapon beneath a huge, two-wheeled cart and towed it slowly up the island's switchback road.

Once at the battery site, the men laid each cannon tube on the ground, then hoisted it into position with a portable tripod derrick known as a "garrison gin." Finally, the gun barrels were slipped onto gun carriages sturdily built of oak. The carriages, fitted with iron wheels, rotated upon wooden platforms capped with metal rails. The cannon could be pivoted 360 degrees to provide maximum angles of fire.

Shortly after mounting, the engineers test-fired each gun to check the strength of mounts and carriages. It was to be three years before Alcatraz fired its cannon in an official capacity, though. In 1858 the island gave a 21-gun salute to arriving British warship *HMS Satellite*. But the army had not yet stationed artillerymen at the fort. Troops from the Presidio must have had the honor of firing this first salute.

The ISLAND CHANGES SHAPE

With South Battery nearly complete, work now proceeded rapidly on North Battery at the opposite end of the island. Unlike South Battery, this fortification and its caponiere were constructed of brick rather than sandstone. Lt. Tower had finally located a brickyard near Sacramento that met the Corps of Engineers' high standards.

The engineers decided to present an additional obstacle at North Battery to any attackers landing on this side of the island. They

extended the walls of this battery far beyond the gun emplacements themselves, and wrapped the scarps all the way around Alcatraz' perimeter to the Guardhouse above the dock, creating a 20-foot high defensive wall that stretched more than 500 feet.

The guardhouse evolved into a considerable defensive work in its own right. Straddling the roadway between the wharf and North Battery, the guardhouse was in reality a small fort provided with its own 15-foot deep dry moat. An oak drawbridge spanned the moat, flanked by gun ports for 24-pound howitzers. Behind the drawbridge the road entered the guardhouse through a sallyport passageway punctuated by rifle slits in both walls and sealed at either end by heavy, iron-studded wooden doors. The roof of the guardhouse had a breast-high parapet wall and firing steps, arranged so that riflemen could fire downward onto anyone trying to cross the moat.

The howitzer rooms on either side of the sallyport also provided space for a guard detail and the Officer of the Day. In the basement under the guards' room was a claustrophobic chamber, accessible only by ladder, which would serve as the fort's jail.

Work finally began in 1857 on a three-story brick barracks atop the south peak of Alcatraz. It had long been planned to place a permanent barracks building for the garrison on the slope immediately above South Battery, but the engineers decided that the very summit of the island, already occupied by the lighthouse, was a much better location. Not only would this site offer sentries an unobstructed view of approaching vessels, but riflemen firing from atop the barracks' roof and through its rifle-slit windows could command the entire perimeter of the island and all the batteries.

Designed to house a company of artillerymen (approximately 100 soldiers) and eight officers in peacetime, more than double that number could be squeezed into the barracks in time of war.

The Citadel, as the barracks came to be known, was constructed at an elevation of 130 feet, just north of the lighthouse. Workers hacked 10 feet off the island's south peak to form a level plateau, then excavated a rectangular pit measuring 150 by 75 feet. This recess, lined with brick, formed a dry moat, and the three-story Citadel itself was erected in the middle of the ditch. The only entrance to the barracks was across two drawbridges providing access to the second story at both ends. The exterior counterscarp walls of the moat were hollowed out for privies, storerooms and cisterns.

Surrounded by its moat and accessible only by drawbridge, the Citadel was intended to be a place of last refuge in case of attack. Within the two-foot thick walls were living quarters for officers and enlisted men, and stores of food, ammunition and water. For the comfort of the officers, privies were provided "in great number." By rationing troops to two gallons of water a day per man, engineers calculated the garrison could withstand a siege of four months.

Never attacked, but frequently remodeled and tinkered with, the Citadel's squat profile dominated Alcatraz's silhouette for more than half a century.

Also in 1857, the first recorded deaths on Alcatraz occurred. Lt. Prime and a civilian supervisor had just finished inspecting a stretch of excavation along the roadway between the wharf and the guardhouse. A few minutes after Prime left, the supervisor heard a tremendous roar and turned in time to see 7,000 cubic yards of rock

collapse onto the road, burying a team of laborers.

After the rescue party cleared away the debris they found the bodies of Daniel Pewter, age 50, a native of Ireland, and Jacob Unger, 25, from Germany. Also recovered was a dead mule, age and identity unrecorded. A coroner's inquest was held and a finding returned: "There can be no blame attached to any parties for the cause of death."

A second slide occurred soon afterward in nearly the same location, this time luckily with no injuries. The continued instability of this slope led to the construction of a defensive wall even more massive than usual between guardhouse and wharf.

When the engineers completed this portion of wall, the entire eastern face of Alcatraz, from the dock to the northern tip of the island, was protected by high scarps — a distance of nearly 1300 feet. The island began to assume the shape that it bears today.

Changes also occurred in the island's personnel. Lt. Tower routinely transferred to Fort Point and was briefly replaced by his former assistant, Prime.

Late in 1858, Prime also received a new assignment and moved to Mobile Bay, Alabama. Completion of the fortress was now entrusted to 2nd Lt. James Birdseye McPherson, 29, recently arrived from New York.

McPherson was less than enthralled with his new life on Alcatraz. In 1859, he wrote to a friend in Delaware:

"This beats all countries for wind I ever inhabited. At 10 o'clock a.m., every day the sea breeze commences and it is no gentle zephyr I can assure you — The dust flies in every direction. The bay is covered with white caps making it worse crossing ..."

And on another occasion:

"Were it not, that being here in charge of this work is very gratifying to my professional pride I should regret the (assignment) deeply, as it is all my pride is scarcely sufficient to keep my spirits up ..."

Now that the construction of the batteries and the mounting of the permanent weapons was nearing completion, Washington appropriated only $30,000 for Alcatraz in fiscal year 1860. McPherson put this money towards finishing the interior of the Citadel, and learned that the fort would receive its first permanent garrison later that same year.

As 1859 closed, McPherson turned over command of the post to Capt. Joseph Stewart and 86 men of Company H, Third U.S.

JAMES BIRDSEYE McPHERSON

Pictured here as a beloved general during the Civil War, McPherson only four years earlier was a lieutenant entrusted with building the fortress at Alcatraz. He hated it.

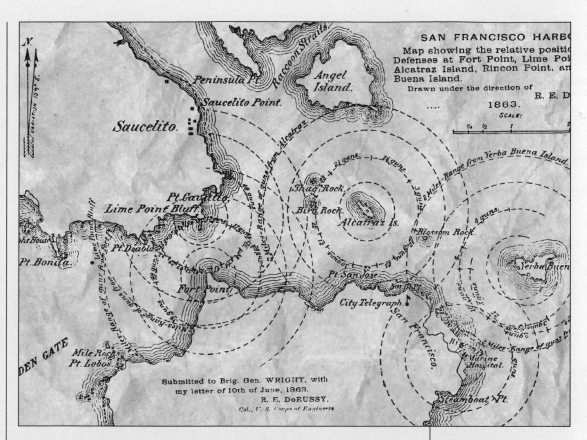

Artillery Regiment on December 30. Hoping to be transferred back East, McPherson must have been gravely disappointed to learn that he was to remain in San Francisco. Even though Stewart was officially in charge of the troops and the completed batteries on Alcatraz, the lieutenant was ordered to stay on and oversee the still-continuing work on the remaining fortifications.

On that cold December day when the Third Artillery arrived, however, eleven anonymous soldiers of Company H came to hold a less-pleasant distinction in the history of Alcatraz. For crimes not recorded in the army files, the men found themselves padlocked in the dim basement prison room of the guardhouse.

"The Post on Alcatraces Island" was open and ready for business, as fortress and prison.

This 1863 defense map of San Francisco Bay clearly shows the overlapping fields of fire from Fort Point, Lime Point and Alcatraz. Proposed secondary batteries on Yerba Buena and the waterfront were never constructed. Angel Island and Point San Jose provided an "inner line" of crossfire. The changing nature of warfare made these plans obsolescent before completion.

THE ALCATRAZ LIGHTHOUSE

With the discovery of gold in 1848 came a flood of "Argonauts" headed for the Sierra goldfields. But the west coast was without aids to navigation, and ships began piling up along the California coast at an alarming rate; within a few months dozens of vessels were sunk or stranded trying to reach the Golden Gate.

With its critical location square in the middle of the bay, Alcatraz Island received top priority for lighthouse construction. Not only was the island a hazard by itself, needing a warning beacon, but ships could use its beam as a range light while entering the harbor, aiming directly for the beacon to maintain a safe course in the middle of the Golden Gate straits.

A shipload of workers and supplies was dispatched to San Francisco, and by mid-December, 1852, a construction gang labored at erecting a lighthouse atop the south peak of the island. The petite, two-storied structure, described as a Cape Cod cottage, contained living quarters for two keepers' families. A stubby light tower rose from the middle of the roof. Capping the tower was an iron and glass lantern room, reached by a spiral staircase.

Construction proceeded swiftly on the lighthouse, but getting the lens itself took longer. The government had gone abroad to find a supplier for Pacific area lighthouses, contracting with the Parisian firm of L. Sautier and Company. Shipped first from France to New

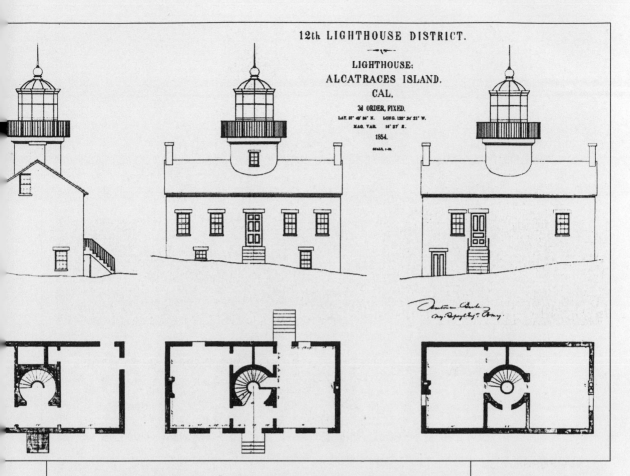

12th LIGHTHOUSE DISTRICT.

LIGHTHOUSE:
ALCATRACES ISLAND.
CAL.
3d ORDER, FIXED.
LAT. 37° 49' 34" N.   LONG. 122° 24' 21" W.
MAG. VAR.   16° 27' E.
1854.
SCALE, 1=20.

York, the Alcatraz lens then made the tortuous Cape Horn passage, arriving in San Francisco in the summer of 1853.

Officially designated a Third Order lens of the Fresnel Pattern, the mechanism was a wonder of 19th Century optics. The hand-ground crystal prisms, set in a brass frame, could gather and focus the light from a whale oil flame until visible 19 miles at sea.

Finding a contractor able to install the delicate apparatus took nearly a year. Just before sunset on June 1, 1854, Principal Keeper Michael Cassin lit the Alcatraz light for the first time.

The lighthouse and the fortress co-existed with few problems. Occasionally, disagreements arose between the two government agencies. When the Lighthouse Board proposed installing a fog bell on the southern slope of the island, the War Department had to agree on a site that would not interfere with the guns of the batteries. And periodically, commanding officers would complain that the grounds and outbuildings of the lighthouse station were 'unmilitary' and detracted from the appearance of the post.

Keepers came and went with great frequency; the average salary of $600 a year was not a great incentive to make a career of lighthouse service. The Treasury Department found a long-term keeper in the mid-1880s when they hired an old sailor, known only as Captain

The original set of plans for the lighthouse on "Alcatraces Island, Cal." As many as three families at once occupied the tiny, isolated quarters.

The lighthouse in the 1890s. By now the original "cottage" has spouted a sizable addition and a post office in the basement. Capt. Leeds holds up a lamppost while an assitant keeper patrols the balcony of the lantern room. In the background is the Citadel, converted to married officers' quarters.

Leeds, who ran the station for many years. The captain put up lattice fencing, planted flowerbeds, kept the buildings white washed, and generally maintained the station in ship-shape fashion. He also ran the island's post office, located in the basement.

In 1908 the army began constructing a massive concrete prison building atop the island. The War Department had some bad news for the light keepers: the lighthouse would have to be moved. The engineers had calculated that when the new prison was complete its walls would rise higher than the lantern of the old light, cutting the lens' visibility by half.

The army suggested a tower directly over the main door to the cellhouse, but the Lighthouse Board had other ideas. In 1909 work began on an 84-foot concrete tower, with spacious living quarters attached to its base for three keepers' families. The lens was moved into the finished tower and relit on December 1, 1909. Three years later, with little fanfare, the 1854 building, first lighthouse on the West Coast, was demolished.

The Alcatraz light remained in service throughout the years of the Disciplinary Barracks and Federal Penitentiary, the civilian keepers

THE ALACATRAZ LIGHTHOUSE

succeeded by Coast Guard personnel in 1939. In 1963, shortly after the closing of the penitentiary, the lighthouse was converted to an automated station.

The lighthouse and its keepers' quarters burned during the Indian Occupation of Alcatraz. On the night of June 2, 1970, a fire of unknown origin broke out atop the island, destroying the doctor's house and gutting the warden's house and lighthouse. The tower acted like a giant chimney, sending a plume of smoke trailing across the bay.

Local mariners received notice that the light was out of service, and the Coast Guard installed a temporary light buoy off the southern tip of the island. Matters became complicated when the occupiers, in a misguided act of public service, hooked up a generator and sporadically operated the old light. When the occupation finally ended, the tower was restored to operation and the ruins of the keepers' quarters demolished.

The Alcatraz light has experienced traumatic changes: its lantern has been replaced three times with more modern technology; its lighting apparatus has evolved from whale oil to kerosene to electricity; and the lighthouse structure itself has been enlarged, overshadowed, rebuilt and ignobly gutted by fire. Despite all the modifications, the Alcatraz light holds the distinction of being the oldest continually operating lighthouse station in the west.

The south fog signal building, circa 1903. The tower-like structure contained a counterweight needed to power a clockwork mechanism that struck the bell with enough force to be heard for miles. The island's two fog bells came under the jurisdiction of the lighthouse keepers, whose duties included winding up the weights several times a day during foggy weather.

THE POST ON ALCATRACES ISLAND

4
CIVIL WAR
1859 — 1868

The plaster was still drying and the interior of the Citadel smelled of fresh varnish and whitewash. The artillerymen of Company H may have had the distinction of being the first troops assigned to the new fort, but the post was far from complete. Stoves weren't yet installed, fireplaces didn't draw right, bunks needed to be constructed, and numerous pieces of artillery were still to be mounted.

Living conditions were less than ideal. McPherson's despised winds blew incessantly each afternoon, scattering sand and dust everywhere. Piles of construction debris littered the island, and water collected in stagnant pools on the exposed rock ledges behind the gun batteries. Adding insult to injury, the local seagull population insisted on building nests on any available open ground. Many an artilleryman tangled with an irate mother gull sporting a four-foot wingspan.

As rumbles of civil war built in the east, the "Post on Alcatraces Island" — for that was its official title — stood completed as the only permanent fortification on San Francisco Bay, or west of the Mississippi River. The fort at Fort Point was still under construction, and Washington continued to dicker with Samuel Throckmorton, latest owner of Lime Point, over what the government considered to be a ridiculously high asking price of $200,000. And the lesser fortifications on Angel Island, Yerba Buena Island and Point San Jose were still only ink-line dreams on engineers' linen maps.

Throughout 1860 and 1861 work continued on expanding existing fortifications on Alcatraz. As talk of secession grew louder, Capt. Stewart's men stepped up the pace in mounting Columbiads and howitzers. Some of the original wooden gun platforms already showed signs of dry rot, so the soldiers also grudgingly dismounted many of the existing cannon and repositioned them atop more permanent granite platforms. Chief of Engineers Totten, still not satisfied with the number of guns mounted on the island, directed Lt. McPherson to build a fifth, then a sixth, gun battery, both facing the Golden Gate.

Military commanders began to fear Southern sympathizers in San Francisco might attempt to storm the arsenal at Benicia and seize

Opposite, a lazy summer day in the 1860s, and the thunder of war is very far away as two artillery officers and their dog lounge on the scrubby grass of Alcatraz. Fog rolls in over the Marin hills in the distance.

arms and ammunition. Their concerns were not unfounded. The clandestine Knights of the Golden Circle, whose membership included many of the local Southern gentry, had developed plans to create a separate "Confederate Republic of the Pacific" in the event of war with the Union.

Even the army's local commander, Kentucky-born Col. Albert Sidney Johnston, was suspect. A giant of a man, Johnston had fought against the Black Hawk Indians, the Mexican Army and rebellious Mormons during his long career. He had even been, briefly, the commander-in-chief of the Army of the Republic of Texas. Nearly sixty and possessing a heavy shock of yellow hair, Johnston became commander of the Department of the Pacific in January, 1861.

The widely reported fact that Jefferson Davis, President of the Confederacy, considered him the finest army officer in the United States did little to build public confidence in Johnston's commitment to defend San Francisco. Rumors flew he was going to allow Southern forces to capture the bay forts.

"There is treason on Alcatraz," read one letter sent to President Abraham Lincoln. *"To insure success of the scheme, Albert Sydney Johnston was placed in command of Fort Alcatraz [sic]. It was arranged that the leaders in San Francisco with a force of picked men sufficient for the purpose, should surprise and capture the fort."*

Johnston was, in fact, approached by local Confederate organizers who sought his assistance in exactly this type of scheme. A delegation of Knights of the Golden Circle was sent to pay a social visit on the colonel and ascertain his political leanings.

One of the delegates, a young firebrand named Asbury Harpending, recorded Johnston's remarks: *"Before we go further, there is something I want to mention. I have heard foolish talk about an attempt to seize the strongholds of government under my charge. Knowing this, I have prepared for emergencies, and will defend the property of the United States with every resource at my command, and with the last drop of blood in my body. Tell that to our Southern friends!"*

Contemporary historians have questioned the exactness of Harpending's version of the colonel's declaration, but Johnston's sworn allegiance to his duty as an officer and a gentleman in the U.S. Army thunder down over the decades. For the moment, any plan to seize San Francisco quietly evaporated.

ALBERT SIDNEY JOHNSTON

Though Col. Johnston upheld the Union in San Francisco, he later became a Confederate general, dying on his horse "Fire-Eater" at the battle of Shiloh.

In February, 1861, in an effort to protect the ordnance stored at the vulnerable Benicia Arsenal, Johnston ordered 10,000 muskets and 150,000 cartridges moved to Alcatraz. When the muskets and ammunition were unloaded at the island dock, they quickly overflowed all available storage areas. In desperation, Capt. Stewart had his artillerymen stack the crates in the halls and bedrooms of the already overcrowded Citadel.

Col. Johnston also ordered Fort Point be immediately garrisoned and rushed to completion, and that its first mounted guns be positioned to defend the fort against a land attack, not naval forces. Stewart on Alcatraz was directed to maintain calm among San Francisco's civilian population, provide troops for additional security at other government installations around the bay, and defend his post against any attempts to seize it.

Stewart also received a command to use extreme caution when challenging suspicious vessels approaching Alcatraz. Col. Johnston ordered that in the event of possible attack, "The sentinel or guard must report (to you) at once. The only conditions on which you will be justifiable in using your arms will arise when an organized attack is made on your post, and of this fact you must be the sole judge." At the same time, however, Stewart was directed not to fire the fort's guns in artillery practice; Johnston didn't want to alarm the local populace.

This last order was shortly rescinded, and in July the Alcatraz artillerymen promptly set fire to Angel Island by lobbing an explosive shell onto its grassy slopes.

Although his sympathies lay with the Confederacy, Col. Johnston continued to carry out his duties faithfully until relieved of command. Informed by Washington that he was finally being replaced, Johnston concealed his orders until his successor, Brig. Gen. Edwin V. Sumner, arrived in San Francisco. Johnston wanted the transfer of command of the Department of the Pacific to take place smoothly and not inflame the Unionist-Secessionist passions of San Francisco. He especially didn't want to create a vacuum of military power during which local Southerners might attempt to capture the bay forts.

Gen. Sumner arrived to take command of the Department of the

The biggest guns mounted on Alcatraz were the ponderous 15-inch calibre Rodmans, which could throw a solid shot or explosive shell 3 miles. This one, mounted on the extreme northern tip of the island, shows the rail-topped granite platform needed to support nearly 60,000 pounds of cast iron.

The map shows the layout of Alcatraz Island with labeled features including:

NORTH BATTERY
HALLECK
HALLECK
MANSFIELD
ROSECRANZ
STEVENS
NORTHWESTWARD EXTENSION OF WEST BATTERY
TOWER
MCPHERSON
WEST BATTERY
MCCLELLAN
SOUTH BATTERY
MCCLELLAN
PRIME
THREE-GUN BATTERY
DOCK
GUARD HOUSE
BOMB-PROOF BARRACKS
PARADE GROUND
CITADEL
LIGHTHOUSE
TEMPORARY BARRACKS

NAMING *THE* BATTERIES

Alcatraz Island was almost totally encircled by guns during the later months of the Civil War. North and South Batteries had been greatly expanded, Three-Gun Battery and West Battery had been completed, new emplacements had been built connecting West and South Batteries, and work was nearly finished on an earthen addition to West Battery mounting 18 guns.

It was all rather confusing. Designations such as "the Extension North-Westward of the West 8-inch Columbiad Battery" did little to clarify things for the Board of Engineers back in Washington, even if they had ordered the fortifications built in the first place. Washington decided to give the batteries new identities, and in 1863 Alcatraz' supervising engineer Lt. George Elliot was ordered to find appropriate names.

Using the then-popular tradition of naming fortifications after military officers, Elliot came up with a list of names that he forwarded to Washington for approval. Since it mattered little during the Civil War whether the honored persons were alive or dead, most of the names Elliot suggested were those of contemporary army officers, several still on active duty. Not surprisingly, all of the proposed names were also members of the Corps of Engineers.

Proceeding counterclockwise from the southern tip of the island, the names finally settled upon were Battery Prime, Battery McClellan, Battery McPherson, Battery Tower, Battery Stevens, Battery Mansfield, Battery Rosecrans and Battery Halleck.

Pacific on April 25, 1861 — the day after the Pony Express arrived with news of the Confederate attack on Fort Sumter. Johnston promptly resigned his commission, returned to Texas and accepted the rank of general in the Confederate Army. Later he would die on the fields of "bloody Shiloh" fighting for the Stars and Bars, becoming one of the great heroes of the Confederacy.

Gen. Sumner immediately issued commands for all military forces in and around San Francisco to go on full alert. He feared either an attack by enemy vessels, an open assault on the forts staged by local Secessionists, or both. In his general orders, Sumner ordered that any ship flying the Rebel flag would "immediately be captured" or "fired into and sunk."

By late April the Alcatraz garrison was composed of Companies A, I, H and M of the 3rd Artillery, a company of engineers, and 42 new recruits for a total of eight officers and 361 enlisted men. The soldiers now far outnumbered the capacity of the two-company Citadel, so the aging wooden laborers' barracks above South Battery were turned into enlisted soldiers' quarters.

Sumner designated Alcatraz the salute post for the harbor, its duties to include greeting arriving ships and challenging unidentified vessels. Standard procedures also were issued for ships entering the harbor. Army regulations ordered that all arriving vessels heave-to under the guns of Alcatraz and wait for the crew of a government cutter to come aboard and check cargo and papers. Once cleared, the ship could then proceed to a mooring along the San Francisco waterfront.

Many local Confederate sympathizers continued to dream of a separate republic in California. Some even laid elaborate plans to speed the day when gold from the Sierra Nevadas would find its way to the coffers of the South. With these unlimited reserves of wealth, they hoped, the Confederacy could indefinitely finance its "War for States' Rights" and gain eventual independence from the Union.

In March of 1863, military intelligence officers learned that a group of Secessionists was converting the schooner *J. M. Chapman* into a privateer. The *Chapman* conspirators' plans were elaborate. The schooner was to be armed with cannon, sail outside the harbor and capture an ocean-going steamship. The steamer, in turn, would be sailed to Mexico, outfitted as a Confederate warship, and then used to raid Yankee commerce in the Pacific.

The Secessionists' fevered schemes also included blockading San Francisco Bay until Confederate forces could capture the city. The plans were eventually discovered, though, when *Chapman's* skipper began talking about the plot in waterfront taverns, apparently under the influence of strong beverage. The military shortly had *Chapman* and her crew under close surveillance.

On the night of her scheduled sailing, *Chapman* was intercepted by the Navy while ignobly stranded on a sand bar awaiting high tide.

THE FLOATING FORTRESS

Washington authorized an additional element of protection in late 1863 when it ordered the Passaic-class monitor USS Camanche, then under construction in New Jersey, shipped to San Francisco. The Navy planned to reassemble the ironclad and put her into commission as a "water battery" backing up the permanent army fortifications on the bay. Her two 15-inch caliber Dahlgren guns would provide a warm surprise for any rebel raiders trying to sneak into the harbor.

Upon completion, Camanche was immediately disassembled, loaded aboard the cargo ship Aquila, and shipped via Cape Horn. Upon arriving in San Francisco, however, on Nov. 14, 1863, Aquila promptly sank at her moorings with the ironclad still stowed in her holds. Camanche thus became the only U.S. Navy ship to sink before she was launched.

Rumors of Confederate sabotage inevitably surfaced among San Francisco residents. Faulty caulking in Aquila's hull, coupled with a freak bay storm and a rugged Cape Horn passage were more realistic explanations. The navy resigned itself to a lengthy salvage

The crew was promptly arrested, the schooner seized and towed to the Alcatraz dock.

Inside the vessel the fort's soldiers found 15 men, two brass cannon, ammunition, and assorted supplies. The leaders of the group were identified as Asbury Harpending, Ridgely Greathouse and Alfred Rubery, prominent San Francisco citizens and former Knights of the Golden Circle. Harpending, the soldiers discovered, possessed

USS Camanche *at anchor off Mare Island in her later years. Monitors barely had three feet of freeboard — the distance between the water and the deck — and could only sail in the calmest water. As a result,* Camanche *stayed well inside the Golden Gate.*

Fall, 1864, and Camanche *is being assembled at Peter Donohue Shipyard in San Francisco. The monitor is nearly ready for launching, but still awaits fitting-out with engines, revolving turret and guns. The ship wasn't actually completed until the Civil War had ended.*

operation, during which Aquila's masts and superstructure were cut away, her waterlogged hull raised, Camanche's components retrieved, and the pieces dried out before the monitor could be reassembled in a local shipyard.

USS Camanche *was finally launched in late 1864 and commissioned on Aug. 22, 1865 — four months after the end of the war. She spent an uneventful peacetime career put-putting around San Francisco Bay, guns used only in occasional target practice, and as a training ship for the California Naval Militia. The little warship was written off at Mare Island in 1899 and ended her days ingloriously, as a coal barge in the backwaters of an Oakland estuary.*

letters signed by Jefferson Davis granting him an officer's commission in the Confederate Navy.

Union forces took the *Chapman* fiasco seriously. Before the night was out, the conspirators found themselves confined in separate cells in the Alcatraz guardhouse, where they would spend the next several weeks undergoing questioning. Eventually tried and convicted of treason (the jury taking only four minutes to return a guilty

Guns in every direction — the view from the roof of South Caponiere shows South Battery and a portion of West Battery, with temporary wooden buildings sitting higher on the island slopes. Litter on the ground and a blurry workman trundling a wheelbarrow tell us work is still in progress.

verdict), only a pardon from President Lincoln saved the three ringleaders from 10-year sentences in the island prison.

Pro-Union citizens of San Francisco now constantly clamored for more defenses for their city. In their imaginations, the Pacific swarmed with Confederate raiders and every darkened window harbored clandestine meetings of traitorous Secessionists. The *Chapman* incident reinforced their worst fears.

Gen. Sumner was replaced as departmental commander in the fall of 1861. His replacement, Col. George Wright, was outraged upon arrival at the lack of adequate bay defenses and the slowness in erecting additional fortifications. He fired off a blistering letter to the War Department:

"I fear greatly that the masterly inactivity system and the time consumed in planning and deliberating as to the best points for our batteries, and then going to work with permanent fortifications, slowness may be fatal [sic]. While we are meditating some morning, the first thing we shall know will be the enemy's guns thundering against the city ... Prompt and energetic action are necessary or we may suffer terribly."

California's military commanders soon pressured Washington into erecting the long-awaited secondary defenses on the bay — the inner line of batteries first envisioned back in 1850. The revised

plans now called for building five temporary gun batteries — two on Point San Jose in San Francisco and three on Angel Island — and further enlarging the fortifications on Alcatraz.

But it appeared that nothing was going to be constructed at Lime Point for a while; the government and Mr. Throckmorton were still almost $100,000 apart in their negotiations over the land.

In late 1863, work finally began on the temporary batteries at Point San Jose and on Angel Island. Much simpler in design than the works on Alcatraz and Fort Point, these batteries were mere depressions scooped out of the ground with a few cannon dropped in place. The three batteries on Angel Island weren't even provided with decent masonry parapets; wooden timbers lined their gun pits. But when these temporary emplacements were complete the inner harbor was protected by crossfires at five different points, all radiating out from Alcatraz Island. Bay residents breathed a little easier.

A DIRECTION so UNUSUAL

The number of soldiers assigned to Alcatraz swelled throughout the Civil War, reaching a high point of 433 men in early 1865. Troops continually arrived, departed, and underwent training before being shipped out to patrol the southwestern frontier. (Few California troops ever saw action on the battlefield.) The tiny parade ground north of the Citadel echoed with the shouted com-

This view of the North Caponiere and North Battery shows Angel Island in the background. Near the doorway is a sling cart, used for moving heavy cannon barrels around the island. Below, the truncated caponiere today. See Area #1 in the Walking Tour on page 155.

mands of noncommissioned officers teaching enlistees close-order drill and the manual of arms. While awaiting battle, island soldiers mounted, dismounted, and shuffled cannon among the batteries.

The Alcatraz garrison was also assigned the duty of manning guns in a new battery under construction at Point Blunt on Angel Island. Road conditions on that island were so poor that it was easier to ferry soldiers over from Alcatraz than have the Angel Island troops march around the perimeter of their own post. In an economy move, the Alcatraz soldiers also cultivated a collection of vegetable patches in a sheltered valley not far from Pt. Blunt known as the "Alcatraz Gardens." The

army found produce grown there to be cheaper than the oft-inflated market prices of San Francisco.

Another invasion scare arose in mid-1863 when intelligence reports arrived that Confederate warships were prowling the Pacific and might try to capture San Francisco. The departmental commander ordered the harbor defense forts to be ready for instant action. On Alcatraz, all batteries were directed to be manned within three minutes of the sounding of the "long roll."

The morning of Oct. 1, 1863, dawned clear and calm, an enjoyable Indian Summer day. The air turned warm and the fort's sentries kept up their monotonous pacing, bothered a little more than usual by the itchy blue wool uniforms they had been issued.

On this particular Thursday the post assumed an additional duty. Revenue cutter *Shubrick* had been called away from its regular station to assist a Russian ship stranded at Point Reyes, so Alcatraz' two small boats were now responsible for rowing out and boarding all arriving ships to clear them for entry into the harbor.

Just about noon, a sentry reported to the Officer of the Day that an armed vessel was entering the Golden Gate not an unusual occurrence, since warships of all nations frequently visited San

THE POST *ON* ALCATRACES ISLAND

Francisco Bay. But the ship's unusual course caught the sentry's attention. Instead of heading for the designated moorage between Alcatraz and Telegraph Hill to await clearance, the ship was being towed by two rowboats and headed for Raccoon Straits on the north side of still unarmed Angel Island. The course led to the Benicia Arsenal and the navy yard at Mare Island.

The officer dutifully reported the sighting to the fort's commander, Capt. William Winder, who decided to have a look for himself. From the top of the Citadel, Winder spotted the ship near Lime Point on the Marin shore.

"I could distinguish a flag flying at her peak, but there being no wind, I could not tell her nationality," Winder later explained. "The ship's direction was so unusual I deemed it my duty to bring her to and ascertain her character."

Winder ordered a blank charge fired from North Battery as a signal to heave to. As the shot echoed over the bay, the strange ship ignored the challenge. The oarsmen in the small boats kept up their measured pace, now towing the vessel past Sausalito.

The captain now made a decision which would have international repercussions. "Apparently not attracting her attention, I directed a

Battery Mansfield, looking south toward the Citadel and Engineers compound. The building at center with the ridged roof housed one of the fort's many ammunition magazines. A lone sentry guards the unfinished barbette mounts and empty iron gun carriages. The long time exposures of these pictures have erased any other inhabitants of this crowded islet.

gun to be loaded with an empty shell and to be fired 200-300 yards in front of her."

For the only time in its history, an Alcatraz gun barked in earnest. A few seconds later a column of water erupted ahead of the warship.

Putting a shot across a ship's bows is a universally recognized signal, and a challenge not argued with. The vessel immediately halted and dropped anchor.

Capt. Winder now found himself in an awkward position. He had challenged and stopped an unidentified (and possibly hostile) warship, but had no way of ascertaining her intent; the fort's two boats were busy inspecting vessels in other parts of the harbor.

For a few minutes the impasse continued, and suddenly the vessel opened fire. The ship let loose a fusillade "and was entirely enveloped in the smoke of her guns." Artillerymen on the island crouched behind their parapets, but no shots slammed into Alcatraz' masonry walls. Winder determined that the warship was answering the island's challenge with a 21-gun salute, an international symbol of recognition.

Alcatraz began to respond with its own salute, but before it could finish Fort Point opened fire as well.

Whether Fort Point was giving its own salute or was actually firing upon the ship has never been determined. But to Adm. John Kingcome aboard *HMS Sutlej,* new Commander-in-Chief of Her Majesty's Naval Forces in the Pacific, paying a courtesy call on San Francisco, the message was clear: his flagship had been fired upon by supposedly friendly forts of a foreign nation.

Kingcome was not amused.

No sooner had the smoke cleared than messages began to fly. *Sutlej* signaled to Alcatraz. Alcatraz signaled *Sutlej.* Fort Point signaled Alcatraz. And Admiral Kingcome eventually vented his displeasure upon Col. George Wright, latest commander of the Department of the Pacific.

Many San Franciscans considered Winder to be the hero of the day, especially considering Great Britain's unconcealed support of the Confederacy. While Col. Wright did his best to smooth ruffled British feathers, he continued to support Winder and his actions on Alcatraz. The departmental commander formally pointed out to Admiral Kingcome that *Sutlej* had not only entered a foreign port in time of war, but his ship had also ignored all established procedures for recognition and mooring, and had failed to respond to a challenge from a military post.

Kingcome's fuming and blustering continued for several days, but eventually *Sutlej* huffily sailed from San Francisco and the episode wore itself out. Had Winder's artillerymen misjudged their gunfire and actually hit *Sutlej,* however, American-British relations might have taken a very different turn. The only rebuke Winder received came in a letter from Col. Wright five months later: "It is

expected that the delicate duty devolving on military commanders will be exercised with prudence."

In 1864, Capt. Winder found himself in much deeper trouble, this time for inviting the commercial photography firm of Bradley and Rulofson onto Alcatraz to make documentary photographs of his post. Winder had been extremely accommodating, and the photographers had been thorough. They made 50 "sterio-scopic size" views of the island, including the Citadel, the dock, the enlisted barracks, and every road and battery in the fort.

Lt. George Elliot, supervising engineer on Alcatraz, was delighted with the results. He forwarded a glowing report to Washington, helpfully including two photographs that illustrated his recent work on the batteries for the Board of Engineers' perusal.

Things quickly turned sour for Winder. Secretary of War Edwin M. Stanton was enraged to learn that not only had the photographs been taken, but they were being made into portfolios and would shortly be available for sale to the general public at $200 a set. The fact that Winder's father was a brigadier general in the Confederate Army did little to increase the captain's credibility with those who questioned his motives for having the photos made. Washington couldn't imagine anything that might help the enemy more.

Once again, the Departmental Commander rose to Winder's defense. Gen. Irvin McDowell, newly arrived, tried to explain to Washington that the captain's motive was not sedition but rather "was one of pride and interest in his important command and a desire to have himself and the command have pictures of the place." Besides, McDowell pointed out, would Winder have acted so openly if his actions had been seditious? No matter. Secretary of War Stanton

The left face of South Battery. Every other gun position is occupied by a Columbiad cannon, with plenty of ammunition and rammer staffs at the ready. The nearest pyramid of cannon balls appears to have been freshly painted, a common fatigue duty for troops. Goat Island is visible in the distance.

MYSTERIOUS VIEWS

Historians researching the history of Alcatraz have long mourned the destruction of the 1864 photo series. So it was thought for 126 years. In the course of researching this book, the author came across a photograph credited to the City of Sacramento showing a battery of Columbiad cannon, labeled simply "Fort Point — the Civil War." The photo seemed odd because it clearly showed an architectural feature that Fort Point never sported — a caponier with flank howitzers.

A few phone calls to Sacramento's archivists revealed this was one of a series of eight photos of a Civil War-era fort which the city had acquired in 1968.

A complete set was ordered, and the photos turned out to be survivors of the long-suppressed series taken by Bradley and Rulofson in the early summer of 1864. The photographs had been donated by the descendents of Henry Burnett, an officer in the California Volunteer Cavalry who was stationed on the island during the war (and who was also the nephew of California governor Peter Burnett). Apparently, the photographs were somehow acquired by the younger Burnett during his enlistment, perhaps even fished out of the trash. At some point, the views had been erroneously identified as Fort Point and had thus eluded researchers for more than a century. The haunting view of the Alcatraz parade ground above, and the pictures on pages 21, 22, 27, 42, 43, 45 and 47 are published here for the first time.

The photographs' reappearance gives a fascinating glimpse of long-vanished fortifications, but they remain something of a mystery. How did these eight images escape the War Department's wrath and subsequent purge of negatives and prints? And where are the remaining 42 views described by Lt. Elliot in his 1864 correspondence? Research continues.

ordered Maj. Gen. Halleck, Chief-of-Staff of the Army, to have the photographs suppressed. The War Department had the negatives and all known prints seized and destroyed.

THE BIG GUNS

The defense of San Francisco was low priority for Washington throughout most of the Civil War. The protection of the capital city and the Atlantic seaboard came first. As the war dragged on, though, the threat of a Confederate naval attack upon Eastern cities decreased and modern ordnance became available for bay forts.

In early 1864 the new guns began to arrive in San Francisco. Some of the batteries on Alcatraz received the most modern smoothbore guns that foundries of the East could produce - streamlined 8-inch and 10-inch Columbiads of an 1861 pattern known to soldiers as "Rodmans" in honor of their designer, Capt. Thomas Rodman of the Ordnance Department.

Most of the existing guns on Alcatraz were 1844 model Columbiads, some of which had demonstrated a frightening tendency to burst upon firing. In 1861, an 8-incher in North Battery exploded during target practice, splitting open like an overripe zucchini and spraying the emplacement with flying iron. The departmental commander subsequently ordered all similar Columbiads manufactured in the same lot as this particular gun be fired only with reduced powder charges, inevitably minimizing their defensive value.

In contrast, Rodman cannon had a reputation for safety that appealed to artillerymen. The Ordnance Department had calculated the pressures that built up inside a gun barrel at the moment of firing, and designed the Rodmans' "water bottle" shape to match that pressure curve. The foundries turning out the guns also prestressed the barrels during the casting process, circulating water through the bore so that the cannon tube cooled from the inside out. Rodmans weren't ornate, but they didn't blow up when a soldier yanked the lanyard.

The fort's grateful artillerymen dismounted many of the old, hazardous Columbiads in the spring of 1864, replaced them with Rodmans and made the obsolete cannon available for ornamental purposes to other military posts and towns around the state. (One of these surplus guns is still found in a playground in Grass Valley, California. When last seen by the author, it was painted green with flowers in its muzzle.)

Nearly 100 guns of various calibers and models had been emplaced on the island when news arrived that three of the largest cannons then in production — 15-inch caliber Rodmans — were being shipped to

Alcatraz. Weighing 50,000 pounds each, these monsters could lob a 440-pound solid shot up to three miles and punch through four feet of oak planking. No warship in existence, not even an ironclad, could withstand the meteoric impact of a direct hit.

The mounting of the first 15-incher took place on July 20, 1864, and the entire Alcatraz garrison participated in the festivities that marked its installation. It was an eventful party. Ten years later, a private named Lorch still retained vivid memories of the day. He told the post's surgeon how "liquor had been freely supplied to the command on that day in celebration of mounting the first 15-inch gun at this fort." So much liquor had flowed, stated Lorch, that casualties occurred. Two privates "while in a state of intoxication fell from an embankment 40 to 50 feet high." Both enlisted men were killed.

The engineers and the fort's commanders had always recognized that the Alcatraz dock was poorly defended. None of the batteries could fire directly onto the wharf, and the defensive wall running to the Guardhouse was designed to be manned only by riflemen during attack.

In the spring of 1865 work began on the last masonry fortification built on the island, a two-story brick battery located behind the dock where the old defensive wall had stood.

Officially titled the "Bomb Proof Barracks," the engineers designed this battery to mount 22 cannon in two tiers of arched brick gunrooms known as casemates. These weapons would fire through embrasures in the 10-foot thick walls, while the roof would be arranged to mount another 10 guns on barbette platforms.

The casemates would also serve as long-needed permanent quarters for the hundreds of enlisted men on the island, most of whom were still crammed into temporary wooden barracks on the southern slopes of the island.

The lower tier of casemates would double as kitchens and mess rooms for the soldiers, while the second tier would contain barracks space for hundreds of enlisted men. It was planned that the troops would eat and sleep alongside their cannons, like sailors in the navy, with bunks and living spaces in the same casemates as the hulking Rodman guns. A maze of small storage rooms, cisterns and privies, dug into the sheer rock hillside behind the casemates, would provide additional space for the enlarged garrison's use.

With some pride, Elliot, now a captain, made his end-of-year report for 1865. He had much to summarize, what with the mounting of the 15-inch Rodmans, the completion of all the barbette batteries, the beginning of work on the Bomb Proof Barracks, and the end of the long war.

He made a calculation for his report. "The weight of metal which could have been discharged simultaneously from Alcatraz on the 30th of June 1864 was 4,549 lbs." By the end of the War, he now figured, the total had increased by more than a ton, to 6,949 pounds.

FILLING UP *THE* GUARDHOUSE

The guardhouse on Alcatraz had become rather crowded by the time the *Chapman* conspirators were imprisoned there in 1863. The island's location in the middle of San Francisco Bay made it considerably more escape-proof than the average stockade, so other army posts began sending their hardcore soldier prisoners to Alcatraz early on for safekeeping. In fact, the fort's first non-garrison prisoner arrived only two months after the fort opened when Pvt. Matthew Hayland arrived — an "insane man delivered for confinement and safekeeping awaiting transfer to Washington."

The practice of shipping hardcore cases to the island fortress became formal on Aug. 27, 1861, when the post was designated as the official military prison for the entire Department of the Pacific.

From 1861 to the end of the war the number of prisoners varied from 15 men to about 50. Not only were soldiers and Confederate privateers sent to the island, but also local citizens and politicians whose loyalties were suspect. Even the Chairman of the California Democratic Committee found his way to Alcatraz after making an 'incendiary' speech during the 1864 Presidential campaign. He was only released after posting a $25,000 bond and swearing an oath of allegiance to the Union.

The earliest prisoners found themselves confined in the bare basement cell room of the guardhouse, let out only for periodic exercise. These men presented something of problem to the fort's commanding officer. Whether army soldiers or civilians, the commander didn't feel he could leave the convicts locked in the basement at all times. As early as 1861, Capt. Stewart requested formal guidance in this matter from the departmental commander. Col. Sumner replied by directing Stewart to use the prisoners "for police purposes," performing maintenance and clean-up work around the post until their sentences were finished.

Before long, an even greater problem arose. By late 1862, so many prisoners had been confined in the guardhouse that they overflowed the single basement cell room and had to be housed in one of the howitzer rooms flanking the sallyport. Capt. Winder reported that the prisoners were occupying so much space, his garrison could not mount the howitzers that were supposed to defend the guardhouse, drawbridge and defensive walls. The fort's security was compromised.

Living conditions for these early prisoners was grim in the extreme. No individual cells had been provided; the men slept together on the bare floors of the dungeon. Blankets were considered a luxury, there was no running water or heat in the cell rooms, and sanitary facilities were almost non-existent. Lice, fleas and vermin multiplied in the prisoners' clothing and hair. The stench must have been staggering. In the fall of 1861 severe outbreaks of illness among the prisoners were reported, and the departmental commander ordered the men be temporarily put into tents so a thorough "cleansing of the prison room." could be carried out.

To relieve the overcrowding and villainous conditions in the guardhouse, Winder erected a temporary wooden prison just north of the sallyport in fall, 1862. The frame building measured roughly 20 by 50 feet and contained two large prison rooms and separate room for the guards. Iron grates were installed over all windows.

This cellhouse, designed only to ease overcrowding for the duration of the war, was the first of dozens of prison structures to be erected on Alcatraz in the coming years.

PEACE IN THE EAST

On April 9, 1865, Robert E. Lee surrendered his Army of Northern Virginia to Gen. U. S. Grant at Appomattox Courthouse. The new transcontinental telegraph ticked out the story of Lee's defeat to an eager San Francisco, and guns from the bay's forts boomed out in celebration. The Alcatraz garrison stood down from the alert status the post had maintained for four years.

Less than a week later, soldiers on the island awoke to receive orders for a new and somber duty. The telegraph had ticked again during the early hours of April 15th, this time bringing news of the assassination of Abraham Lincoln.

Artillerymen from Alcatraz were ordered into San Francisco to maintain order and prevent possible rioting. Emotions ran hot, and the government feared unrepentant Confederates might demonstrate in celebration of the president's death. Together with troops from the Presidio, Alcatraz soldiers coordinated efforts with the San Francisco police to take "such measures as will preserve the peace of the city."

There was violence on the afternoon of the 15th. Crowds of Unionists sacked pro-Confederate newspaper offices in the city, and that evening scores of street-corner fires burned late into the night. And throughout California there were men "so utterly infamous as to exult over the assassination of the President." These men were immediately taken into custody before the mobs could reach them. In

the two weeks between April 17th and June I st, the military arrested 68 men around the state for their treasonous rejoicing. Alcatraz received 39 of these prisoners.

The City of San Francisco entered a period of official grief. On April 19th soldiers marched in the presidential funerary procession down Montgomery Street. From Alcatraz, a half-hourly cannon shot rang out over the Bay - the fort's batteries being given the honor of sounding San Francisco's official mourning toll.

A reporter visited Alcatraz during the summer of 1865 and chronicled the fate of Secessionists still imprisoned on the island. He recorded the men were having the treason sweated out of them by working eight to 12 hours a day excavating the site of the Bomb Proof Barracks. To restrict their movements, they had been shackled to 6-foot chains attached to 24-pound iron balls.

The prisoners labored under the supervision of an armed guard and, frequently, under the mortifying gaze of women residents and visitors on the island. If they chose not to work, the convicts were put on a diet of bread and water and confined in a "sweat box" barely high enough inside to stand erect. The reporter took pains to describe how the prisoners drank coffee made from used coffee grounds.

The end of the Civil War also marked the end of Alcatraz' principle role as a harbor-defense post. Lessons painfully learned during the war had shown the vulnerability of looming masonry forts. A new era of military technology rendered Alcatraz's brick and granite fortifications obsolescent.

Although work continued half-heartedly on modernizing the old batteries for several more years, it was the fetid little prison building down by the guardhouse that foreshadowed the future of the island. It would shortly become the nucleus of a sprawling complex of firetrap cellblocks, wooden stockade walls, and reinforced concrete cellhouses that, by the early 20th century, would cover a third of Alcatraz and obscure almost all traces of fortifications.

Fortress Alcatraz at its zenith, with newly constructed ramparts overlooking the bay and bristling with cannon. Behind the fortifications are whitewashed barracks, stables and workshops; atop the hill, the Citadel and lighthouse. The island's soft profile is already beginning to harshen — compare to the photograph on page 14.

HELIOS *AND THE* ISLAND FORTRESS

"All right, gentlemen. Please be very still!"

The photographer uncapped the twin brass lens casings on his hulking stereoscopic camera. Soldiers gathered in the late-afternoon sun held their collective breaths for the seconds-long exposure.

"Done! Thank you!"

The troops relaxed from their awkward poses, but master photographer Eadweard Muybridge had preserved the artillerymen of Battery McClellan for posterity: two soldiers ramming home a powder charge with a 20-foot staff, four men hoisting a 15-inch cannonball, two men carrying a wooden pass-box containing a bag of powder for the next shot, the gun pointer straddling the bulbous breech of the weapon, and the Chief of Piece pointing westward toward an imaginary enemy sailing though the Golden Gate.

The year was 1869 and Muybridge had been given free run of Alcatraz. The military had lifted the ban on photography imposed during the Civil War, when then-commanding officer William Winder had outraged Washington by inviting photographers onto the island. This time, the photographer was taking pictures with the full blessing of the United States Army, and actually working with the War Department. His photos would serve as a permanent record of the island fort.

That summer, Muybridge became a frequent visitor on the post. The photographer seemed fascinated with the 15-inch Rodman guns on Alcatraz. He took five different views of the 15-incher in Battery McClellan alone, as intrigued with the distant skyline of San Francisco as with the impressive scale of the highly lacquered cannon.

He also photographed the cannon in Batteries Rosecrans and Prime. Perhaps Muybridge was aware of public interest in state-of-the-art weapons mounted on the secretive fortress.

But Muybridge also took pictures of the Citadel, the minuscule formal garden with the post's officers and families, the wharf, the ordnance yard, the rocky west face of the island, and numerous informal poses of soldiers lounging around the cliffs and batteries. Stereoscopic views of Alcatraz would sell nicely.

Eyes clamped tight against the midday sun, island officers and their families pose stoically in the Citadel gardens. The latticework fence in the background offered scant protection from winds sweeping the post.

Born Edward James Muggeridge in 1830, he had emigrated from England to California in 1852 and settled in boomtown San Francisco. Changing his name to what he considered its proper Saxon spelling, Muybridge proceeded to build a reputation as a pioneer photographer.

He christened himself "Helios: The Flying Studio," and in the age of staid salon photographers, made a point of traveling with a portable darkroom and chronicling the remote "curiosities" of the west: the Yosemite Valley, the tall trees of the Sequoia groves, and the wilderness expanses of Alaska.

In 1869, Muybridge received permission to document military installations around San Francisco Bay. In addition to his Alcatraz series, he also photographed the batteries at Fort Point and Point San Jose, the troops and buildings of the Presidio of San Francisco, and the tiny army post on Yerba Buena Island. The government liked his work, and the Treasury Department later contracted with Muybridge to shoot the lighthouses at Point Bonita, Point Reyes, and the Farallone Islands.

As long as security wasn't compromised, Muybridge could sell sets of the photos to the public.

At the time of his Alcatraz series, though, Muybridge's greatest work still lay in the future. In 1872, he would settle a bet for California Governor Leland Stanford by taking a sequential series of photographs of a trotting horse. One photo showed that all four hooves left

EADWEARD MUYBRIDGE

Without this famous photographer's interest in Alcatraz, much of what we know about 19th-century life at the fortress would be lost.

Here are the same Alcatraz residents, with equally studied poses. The tiny garden is decorated with a picket fence and cannonballs atop pipes. In the middle distance is a row of cannonballs in the ordnance yard.

the ground simultaneously — ending an age-old debate and winning a reported $25,000 wager for the governor.

Muybridge refined this stop-action technique in the 1880s and produced an exhaustive portfolio entitled "Animal Locomotion," recording the movements of hundreds of human and animal subjects. Muybridge's work came to be considered the prototype of modern motion-picture technology.

Yet another view of the ordnance yard, with cannon balls and Rodmans all racked up, the garden and Citadel just visible to the left. These pictures were likely all taken the same day.

Two views of the same 15-inch Rodman cannon in Battery McClellan, taken in 1869. In the background is San Francisco and Telegraph Hill – what appears to be a forest on the far shore are the masts of ships moored along the waterfront.

This Rodman is trained on the Golden Gate, which brackets the horizon three miles away. The island's Rodman guns could just reach any ship entering the bay. At left is a view of Alcatraz taken from a pleasant boardwalk around Point San Jose on the city's north waterfront.

REBUILDING *THE* ISLAND

6

Eadweard Muybridge did a masterful job of documenting the post-Civil War fort on Alcatraz. His photographs gave the public an inspiring impression of gleaming firepower and starched soldiers standing vigilant guard in the heart of San Francisco Bay. His stereographic view cards of the island fortress were widely reproduced, and they turned up in refined Victorian parlors of the era.

But he intentionally neglected to photograph the less picturesque areas of the island — ramshackle sheds and lean-tos that served as offices and kitchens for the garrison, temporary soldiers' quarters above Battery McClellan, and the prison compound. Muybridge probably figured that stereoscopic views of these areas would have minimal commercial appeal.

What the military also did not want publicized was that, since the end of the war, Alcatraz had been obsolete. Hundreds of yards of scarp walls, caponieres and sunken roadways had been rendered useless by advances in siege craft and artillery during the Civil War. The island's vertical masonry walls presented inviting targets for long-range rifled cannon fire of the type that had conquered Fort Pulaski and nearly leveled Fort Sumter. The U.S. Army already had its engineers developing plans to remodel the entire island.

Even the long-awaited Bomb Proof Barracks above the wharf stood unfinished, engineers having determined it would be of minimal defensive value during an assault. When work was suspended in 1867, only the first level of casemates had been completed. The brick arches and piers of the second tier had risen only five feet above the floor. Cannons had not even been emplaced in the few finished gunrooms.

In 1866 the island reached its high-water mark as a fortification; 111 pieces of heavy artillery were mounted in the batteries and eighteen spare cannon rested in the ordnance yard. But most of these weapons were obsolete. Except for the five 15-inch Rodmans and a handful of rifled Parrott guns, the fort's armament consisted of short-range, smaller-caliber smoothbores, now recognized to be ineffective against ironclad warships. Modern warfare demanded bigger

A solitary guard atop the newly built Lower Prison hints at how things changed after the Civil War. Could the sentry box be the same one in the 1864 view of the caponiere on page 43?

Photo 14

Cups and condiment bottles on the tables — virtually the only thing remaining from the prison mess hall is the wall to the left, actually a portion of the 1850s defensive wall, now exposed to the elements on the north side of Alcatraz — see Area #F in the Walking Tour on page 154.

weapons, and the Ordnance Department in Washington recommended in the future only 15-inch and 20-inch caliber smoothbore guns be mounted in the nation's seacoast forts, Alcatraz included.

The most serious shortcomings in Alcatraz' design had been dictated by the island's topography. Steep slopes of natural rock backed nearly all of the batteries, and the army's senior engineer for the Pacific Coast concluded that any projectile hitting these cliffs would shower gun emplacements and artillerymen with a devastating hailstorm of rock splinters. He speculated officers wouldn't be able to force soldiers into some of the batteries during battle. The cliffs would have to go.

In 1868 the task of redesigning Alcatraz was entrusted to Maj. George Mendell of the Corps of Engineers. Studies of the war had led Mendell and other engineers to the conclusion that brick and stone walls were not sufficient protection against rifled cannon fire. Military planners now deemed low-profile earthwork batteries, constructed of vast amounts of soil and sand, preferable for absorbing the impact of modern projectiles.

Mendell's recommendation for Alcatraz was simple and awesome: level the peaks and slopes of the island, spread the resulting

The sallyport through the original guardhouse, with the beamed ceiling supporting the prison library. Beyond the far portal the road continues under the wooden cellblocks. The same area today only misses the cellblocks — see Area #D in the Walking Tour on page 153.

spoil in front of the old scarp walls, and ring the island with Rodman guns and Parrott rifles in earthwork batteries.

He had a ready source of labor — military prisoners.

WORK BEGINS *Again*

In 1869, Mendell forwarded his plans to Washington for approval. The Chief of Engineers cautioned the major that the Board of Engineers was developing new, standardized designs for earthwork batteries and that these plans would be ready shortly. No permanent alterations should be undertaken yet on Alcatraz.

Never one to waste time, Mendell figured he could at least begin leveling slopes on the island. He approached the post commander,

Capt. James Robertson, and obtained permission to use military prisoners for the hard labor of cutting and hauling rock.

The post prison then housed more than 100 men, and Robertson considered about half of them of "sufficient character" to be allowed to work on the fortifications. As an incentive to their efforts, Robertson informed the prisoners the army would commute the sentences "of such men as earn good reputations as laborers."

The work was strenuous. Mendell initially gave his labor parties the task of cutting back the steep slopes at the north end of the island. Using picks, shovels and wheelbarrows, the prisoners excavated and carted away thousands of cubic yards of stone from the cliffs behind Battery Halleck and North Caponiere.

REBUILDING *THE* ISLAND

The easiest way to dispose of the rock debris was simply to toss it over the walls in front of the gun batteries. The convicts constructed ramps leading to the edges of the parapets, and dumped innumerable barrowloads of rock over the sheer masonry scarp walls. This disposal had the additional benefit of permanently burying the 20-foot-high walls and protecting them from enemy gunfire.

When the slopes were reduced to an angle that satisfied Mendell, he ordered topsoil barged over from Marin County and the Presidio. Prison crews trundled the dirt to the excavation sites and covered the freshly cut hillsides with imported soil. The earth was then sown with grass and alfalfa seed to offer minimal protection against erosion.

After six months of experience in employing prisoners, Mendell

Alcatraz' primary mission, however, remained the defense of the Golden Gate. These 15-inchers at the southernmost tip of the fortress were equipped with cranes for hoisting shells.

waxed less than poetic about their abilities: "The men are not industrious and they are careless and at times malicious in their treatment of public property." But they were cheap. "With all these drawbacks there is some profit in employing them." The work continued.

Mendell and the Board of Engineers in Washington continued to exchange design proposals for the new batteries, finally coming to a consensus at the end of December 1869. The definitive plans forwarded to Alcatraz reflected a nation-wide standardization in battery design and armament. The features of this "Plan of 1870" would be repeated at seacoast forts all over the country. Except for some constraints of topography, Alcatraz' new works would be true to the plan. The army proposed 40 Rodmans, all 15-inchers, as sole armament for the island.

In order to provide maximum protection for the guns, the weapons would no longer be mounted in the long, unbroken lines of platforms built in the 1850s. It was planned to emplace the Rodmans in pairs, and each pair would be separated by artificial earth hills called traverses. The traverses would protect against incoming enemy shells and limit any battle damage to, at most, two weapons at a time. Each traverse was also to contain a powder magazine for ammunition. Brick-lined tunnels through the earthworks permitted the safe movement of men and supplies during battle.

Mendell calculated it would cost $323,400 to completely remodel Alcatraz, even economizing by using prison labor on less-skilled portions of the work. He also calculated that from the time work began on the island in 1853 up through the end of 1869 the government had already spent $1,601,677 on the fortifications on Alcatraz — more than five times the engineers' original estimate. It would all have to be rebuilt.

One of Mendell's earthwork batteries on the site of old Battery McClellan — compare to the view on page 58. A gun carriage lies upside-down in the unglamorous, unarmed emplacement.

REBUILDING *THE* **ISLAND**

Alcatraz, then and now.

RESHAPING *THE* ROCK

Engineers began to reshape Alcatraz nearly as soon as they arrived in 1853. Early efforts, however, focused on terracing slopes for gun emplacements and levelling the island's two peaks to clear space for the Citadel, lighthouse, ordnance yard and parade ground. During the Civil War, rock debris removed from higher slopes was piled against many of the scarp walls to protect them from enemy fire.

The post-Civil War years brought the greatest changes in the island's topography.

Convict labor gangs who cut back the slopes behind the batteries repeatedly threw the tailings in front of the remaining scarp walls and inadvertantly extended much of the shoreline of the island. Maj. Mendell dramatically increased the scale of this work when he began rebuilding the defenses according the "Plan of 1870." His work crews cut nearly 30 feet off Alcatraz' northern peak and filled in most of Pirate's Cove.

When Mendell turned his efforts to excavating a vast parade ground, prisoners pushed the broken rock in front of the parapet walls of Batteries Prime and McClellan, burying completely the rocky slopes of the southern tip of the island. In the process, the laborers completely filled in the jagged southern shore between the batteries and the wharf, leaving the southern tip of Alcatraz with its current semi-circular outline.

The western slopes of the island became the site of major quarrying operations in the early 1900s. Pirate's Cove vanished when a seawall was built across the mouth of the deep inlet and backfilled with rubble.

By 1910, Alcatraz' angular, battleship-like profile bore little resemblance to the tiny, humpbacked island surveyed during the Mexican-American War.

LIFESTYLES *OF THE* ENLISTED *AND* INCARCERATED

Convicts rebuilding the Alcatraz defenses were housed in an ever-expanding prison complex growing around the old guardhouse. The wooden Civil War-era cellhouse with its two large cell rooms had been torn down in 1867 and rebuilt on the same floor plan, but this time in more permanent brick. The new structure had three tiers of individual, closet-sized cells, each measuring 3 1/2 by 6 feet and fitted with a solid wooden door. Fresh air trickled from thin gaps at the top and bottom of the doors and through air pipes let into the rear walls of the cells. Beds had not yet been adopted; prisoners slept on pallets on the floor.

In 1868, additional cellhouse wings began to be added as the prison population increased. Two long, barn-like wooden cellblocks were erected on the north side of the guardhouse, cantilevered over the road and engulfing the brick prison. Sometime around 1870 the prisoners also constructed a brick, two-story workshop and recreation hall spanning the roadway on the south side of the guardhouse. The main floor held a chapel and library for the use of both the convicts and the regular garrison soldiers, while a tailor shop for prison workers occupied the top floor.

The construction of the cellhouses and library wing had the unintended effect of giving the roadway an overhead ceiling (in reality, the floors of the cellblocks overhead) for more than 250 feet; riding along the road was like passing through a covered bridge. The

Inside the wooden cellblocks of Lower Prison; three tiers of closet-sized cells and a single pot-bellied stove for heat. Whitewash and black iron were the decor colors of choice.

1857 guardhouse now formed the core of the prison complex, its old howitzer rooms ominously titled "Dungeons."

Soldier-prisoners continued to arrive in ever-increasing numbers from all over the West. The army culled the worst thieves, deserters, rapists, chronic drunkards and repeated escapees from its ranks and sent them to the island fortress. Convicts were not considered fit to wear the regular uniform of the United States Army, so upon arrival prisoners received obsolete or condemned uniform items stripped of insignia and trim. Even brass buttons had been removed and replaced with simple horn ones. Later, a white "P" was emblazoned on the backs of shirts, hats and jackets.

The north shore, then and now, included the library and old guardhouse, and, sticking out over the water, a latrine — see Area #C in the Walking Tour on page 152.

Guards roused the prisoners at 5 a.m. each day, led them from their cells and fed the population en masse in a long, shed-like mess hall along the face of the defensive wall below the cellblocks. Time was then allowed for personal hygiene in a primitive bathhouse and latrine on pilings perched over the cold waters of San Francisco Bay. The post surgeon considered the drafts coming up through the open toilet holes to be a serious health hazard to the prisoners. (One prisoner fell through by accident.)

Men assigned to work on fortifications were then broken into details and led to the gun batteries where the never-ending tasks of demolition and excavation continued. More fatigue parties reported to the dock for transportation to other military posts around the bay. Work details at Point San Jose and the Presidio became especially popular; escape attempts from these mainland assignments were frequent and often successful.

Men not considered trustworthy enough to work outside the prison compound were given simple maintenance tasks, assigned work in the post's small tailor shop, or simply confined in the halls of the cellblocks.

Prisoners not otherwise assigned apparently had the freedom to roam at will about the post, and only the quarters of the fort's regular garrison were considered to be off limits. The sight of

surly, unkempt convicts lounging around the dock offended the military sensibilities of many visiting officers.

A number of prisoners, although considered dependable enough to be given work duties, still had to undergo additional and continuing punishment for their original crimes. These men were chained to 24-pound iron cannon balls, which they either dragged or toted wherever they went. The prisoners commonly referred to this form of penance as "carrying the baby."

It was still the era of corporal punishment in the army, despite regulations adopted to the contrary. Officers at remote army posts sometimes administered floggings, and records show that many prisoners arriving on Alcatraz had been branded with the letters "D" or "T," for the crimes of desertion or thievery. The records are moot, however, if these punishments also took place on Alcatraz.

With few exceptions, army records of individual prisoners during the 1860s and early '70s are virtually non-existent. These were the men who were sent to Alcatraz, lived, worked, served their sentences, departed the island or died there with little formal documentation. Most appear only as statistics on annual post returns prepared by various commanding officers. It was these nameless men who physically transformed Alcatraz Island during decades to come.

The road leading from Lower Prison to the north end of the island bears little resemblance today to its military prison appearance at top — see Area #E in the Walking Tour on page 154.

THE THIRD OF JULY REVIEW AND NAVAL ENGAGEMENT.

THE SHAM BATTLE AT THE PRESIDIO

THE ROCK

The United States was a century old, and the citizens of San Francisco planned to give the country a memorable party. The organizers scheduled a series of gala parades, concerts and speeches for the days leading up to the Centennial. The highlight would be a grand demonstration of military might, a Great Sham Battle planned for July 3, 1876. Cavalry and infantry maneuvers would take place in the Presidio, while out in the bay, army and navy gunners would have opportunity to show their shooting skills.

The *Daily Alta California* had a spasm of purple prediction, building up anticipation for "The Grand Feature":

"The air will be filled with wild screeching shells; dark dense columns of smoke will be seen curling heavenward from ships and batteries; balls of fire will go shrieking like rushing meteors toward the objects of attack; bursting bombs will rend the air with the thunder and roar of battle; and make the wild wave and solid earth quake with terror."

Spectators gathered early on the morning July 3 to secure vantage points atop city hills — the *San Francisco Chronicle* reported 50,000 spectators in the Presidio alone. Chartered steamboats vied for the best anchorages in the bay, while specially invited guests on Alcatraz found perches atop the Citadel roof and on the traverses between the cannon batteries.

Two targets had been selected for destruction. The army forts would direct their fire at a large flag fluttering over a painted rock at Lime Point on the Marin shore, and the navy would have the opportunity to demolish an old scow schooner moored between Lime Point and Alcatraz. The aging vessel had been packed with explosives and combustibles soaked in coal oil, and its silhouette had been altered by the addition of a false turret, so that it looked (at a great distance and if one squinted hard enough) something like a monitor-type ironclad. Its destruction by lethal gunfire from three warships promised to be a sight to behold.

The bombardment begun at 11:30 a.m., when Fort Point loosed a round at the flag on the opposite side of the Golden Gate, more than

The "Great Sham Battle" didn't live up to the great expectations promised by newspapers of the period, but thousands of people showed up anyway.

a mile away. Within minutes, guns from Alcatraz, Angel Island and Point San Jose joined in, beating the water around the target into froth. Observers reported several hits on the slopes near the flag.

Now the navy opened up on the incendiary monitor. Warships *Pensacola, Jamestown* and *Portsmouth* took turns; columns of water erupted around the scow.

Despite thunderous applause from the packed hillsides, the target floated unscathed. A bonus of $20 was quietly offered to the first navy gunner to score on the target. Seventy rounds later, the bonus was still unclaimed. One fellow stated that, for $20, he'd go aboard the target ship and spend the day.

The land forts, satisfied that the flag at Lime Point had been subdued, turned their sights on the scow. Alcatraz' four 15-inch Rodmans fired repeatedly, with all rounds falling well away from the target. A moment of drama was achieved when a wooden packing sabot from a powder charge flew out of the muzzle of one cannon and ricocheted among the soldiers of the battery directly below, tearing away part of one man's uniform and nearly decapitating a non-commissioned officer.

Gunners complained that they were allowed only to fire individual rounds at the target. A real target, said they, would fold from the shock wave of an enormous salvo from the fort batteries. It was a moot point. After a dozen or so rounds, the army guns ran out of ammunition.

More than a hundred rounds had been fired, and the faux monitor remained intact. By now, military embarrassment was acute. *Pensacola* fired a volley of blanks in the direction of the target, and under cover

of the resulting smoke, a young officer was dashingly dispatched in a tug to set fire to the hulk. Most of the now-quiet crowd caught on to the ruse, but one woman spectator in the crowd commented in swooning terms on the soldier's bravery. "Madam," replied another observer, a veteran of the Civil War, "with shooting like that, he's in the safest place in town."

The officer lit the fuses aboard the scow, and the target and its explosive cargo finally disappeared in an inglorious — and anticlimactic — pyrotechnic display.

By the 1890s, Alcatraz bustled with Victorian structures, looking like a little city.

Another spectator, described by the *Chronicle* as a "grizzled veteran," huffed, "If I had a boy 14 years old who couldn't hit that target, I'd wring his neck."

If the sham battle had disappointed the spectators on Alcatraz, they could at least look forward to liberal refreshments provided by the island's commanding officer. But, after leaving their viewing areas, the guests were dismayed to find that military prisoners had broken into the commander's reception room and made off with "a quantity of distilled liquors." The guards eventually located the perpetrators on a secluded beach, far gone in a patriotic stupor.

A reporter on the island, witnessing the artillerymen's poor performance, filed a somewhat apologetic story: "The batteries at Alcatraz are being remodeled and the few guns are smooth bores, which, accurate enough for short ranges, fail in the longer ones."

What no one had informed the journalist was that all appropriations for construction work on Alcatraz had ceased. No more remodeling would ever take place on the island's tunnels and batteries. Congress had cut off all allocations for constructing the nation's fortifications, entering into a period of austere army appropriations that continued until the early 1890s.

Infantry officers and their wives take their air on the Alcatraz dock, as the Army steamer General McDowell *noses in behind them.*

Alcatraz stood only partially complete as fortress. A mere five guns were mounted on the entire post (106 fewer than a decade before), and little more than initial excavation work had been carried out on the six earthwork batteries planned for the southern sides of the island. A turning point had been reached in the fort's history, although no one recognized it at the time. Alcatraz' days as a harbor defense installation were numbered, and its role as a military prison would now take priority.

Maj. Mendell continued to use his paltry annual maintenance budgets for repairing and repainting those few batteries completed in the preceding six years. Unhampered by allocations, though, was his ability to use prison labor to reshape the island. Looking forward to the day when money would again become available, Mendell had the convicts put to work cutting away the southern-facing slopes between the Citadel and old South Battery. The major's justification was that he was creating a parade ground for the post's garrison rather than excavating for new gun batteries. According to another military source, the goal was to reduce Alcatraz's twin summits to a single flat plateau.

Between 1870 and 1876, convict workers carried out the nearly unimaginable task of slicing away the entire southern third of the island, reducing its summit from a height of 125 feet to a uniform elevation of 60 feet. Once again, they carried out most of the work with pick and shovel, the only modern technology being the use of temporary tracks and rail carts for the removal of the rubble. The prisoners dumped the excavated material in front of the old defensive

walls, this time burying the 1850s "blue stone" scarps built by Lts. Tower and Prime, along with what remained of the South Caponier, which, like North Caponier, had been cut down to half its original height during the modernization program. Excavations stopped around 1876, leaving Alcatraz with its present shovel-nosed profile.

SENTENCES *FOR* SOLDIERS

Throughout these last years of the 19th century, the prison population averaged 100 convicts. The offenses of the men confined on Alcatraz represented a cross-section of the crimes 19th-century soldiers were capable of committing. Many prisoners ended up on the island for relatively simple offenses such as stealing or desertion (usually on a repeated basis), while others were sent up for felonious assault, rape, manslaughter and murder.

The army divided the prison population into two categories: general prisoners and military convicts. General prisoners were those who had sentences to serve, but were still considered soldiers in the army; at the expiration of their sentence they would go back to regular duty. Military convicts, by comparison, had received dishonorable discharges, and at the end of their stay on Alcatraz would be given a suit of clothes, $5 in cash, and released directly into society. More than a few of this latter group would try to re-enlist under an assumed name; the only home they knew was military service.

Sentences averaged five years, occasionally ranging up to 20

Chief Lomahongyoma and 18 other Hopi "hostiles" from Arizona who resisted Bureau of Indian Affairs efforts to set up a tribal-farming system. When the Indians arrived on Alcatraz, Jan. 3, 1895, the commanding officer was shocked at their clothing and immediately ordered them into uniform items, in this case, army blouses, trousers, shoes and campaign hats. Lomahongyoma was allowed to keep his chief's blanket and sash as badges of rank.

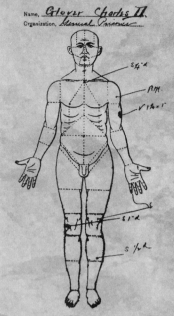

Name. *Glover Charles D.*
Organization. *General Prisoner*

YOU'RE OUT OF THE ARMY NOW

Standards in the post-war army were not especially high, and recruiters frequently overlooked mental problems to bring regiments up to strength. Many convicts were listed as feeble-minded or insane. Army records become more specific after 1870 regarding these individual prisoners, their crimes and sentences. Some of the island's more notable — and notorious — residents included:

Charles Emhoff, *23rd Infantry; deserter — five years confinement at hard labor, wearing the ball-and-chain. Employed on the post dump. A good laboring man, but untrustworthy.*

Samuel McCullough, *1st Cavalry; deserter — five years confinement at hard labor, wearing the ball-and-chain. Dishonorably discharged and drummed out. Marked indelibly with the letter "D." (Probably a tattoo; branding was outlawed in the 1870s) Employed as a baker.*

William Grant, *1st Cavalry; deserter and thief — five years and dishonorable discharge. Placed in solitary confinement for three days on bread and water for assaulting a fellow prisoner in the mess hall.*

Charles Camp, *21st Infantry; deserter — placed in cell on bread and water for refusing to work. Released to rock pile, again refused to work. Placed in dungeon for seven days. Released, later reported for filthiness of person. Prisoner was scrubbed, then on two other occasions was washed with a hose for two-and-a-half and four minutes respectively.*

David Allen, *23rd Infantry; deserter — "A rascal. Swindled the Catholic Priest out of $75 after his discharge."*

Dennis J. Daly, *Jr., 1st Cavalry; deserter — "A perfectly worthless character. An excellent penman."*

John Long, *12th Infantry; deserter and thief — one year. Stationed on Angel Island after discharge, deserted again taking several hundred dollars entrusted to him by officers and enlisted men. Recaptured in San Francisco and returned to Alcatraz to await trial. Hanged himself in his cell. No friends or relatives.*

James Wright, *4th Artillery; deserter — two years. Escaped from work party in San Francisco, found in a Benicia hotel room with a 15-year-old girl. Arrested and taken to Presidio of San Francisco, he again escaped. Still at large in 1879.*

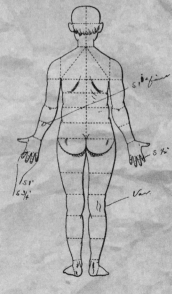

Like other prisoners, Charles D. Glover of the Signal Corps had his scars and birthmarks cataloged. His crime was "embezzlement of moneys received for commercial telegrams and neglect of duty…" while stationed in the Philippines. Poor health sent him to Alcatraz.

Inside the enlisted soldiers' barracks above the dock, with squared-away bunks and racks of rifles, 1893.

years for the most serious offenders. One bit of trivia faithfully noted by the army was that most men had acquired tattoos before coming to Alcatraz. The most popular motif was a dancing girl, closely followed by the goddess of liberty, and then star patterns.

Prisoners were broken into three classes. First Class prisoners had the highest standing and were closest to discharge. They served on desirable work details and enjoyed the greatest degree of freedom in the prison. Third Class men, by contrast, were at the lowest level of privilege, not allowed to work on details off island, and frequently confined to their cells. Their common form of labor was cleaning mortar from reclaimed bricks, and turning big rocks into little ones on the rock pile. For awhile, regulations required Third Class to wear yellow trim of some type on their uniforms, and they were referred to by other prisoners as "the yellow bands."

Second Class prisoners stood midway in the prison hierarchy; these men didn't enjoy the full privileges of the First Class, but neither did they endure the tight security of the "yellow bands." Soldier-prisoners routinely found themselves assigned to Second Class when they first arrived on Alcatraz. Their subsequent conduct determined whether they moved up or down in the class categories.

Alcatraz continued to serve as a place of confinement for special prisoners. Army subjugation of Native American tribes was being carried out in earnest, and bewildered Indian warriors soon found their way to the military prison. Their tiny wooden cells were worlds removed from the western deserts and plains where they had carried out guerilla warfare against the United States. The government incarcerated at least 32 Native Americans in the prison, including several of the army's own Indian Scouts, convicted on

various charges of mutiny.

The first recorded Indian prisoner was known only as Paiute Tom, from Nevada. His stay on the island was brief; he arrived on Alcatraz on June 5, 1873, and was shot dead by a guard two days later, presumably while trying to escape. The next were Barncho and Sloluck, members of the Modoc tribe of northeastern California, who had waged a protracted war against the United States.

Convicted of conspiracy in the murder of Brig. Gen. E. R. S. Canby during peace negotiations in 1873, the two Indians had their death sentences commuted to life imprisonment by presidential order; the army hanged four other Modocs at Fort Klamath, Oregon, for their participation in the same incident. Barncho died of scrofula on May 28, 1875, and was buried on nearby Angel Island. (When Angel Island closed in 1946, Barcho was disinterred and today is

buried in Golden Gate National Cemetery in San Bruno, California, Section E, Lot 357.)

Sloluck was transferred in 1878 from Alcatraz to Fort Leavenworth, Kansas, en route to join his exiled people in Indian Territory. His five-year incarceration is notable as the longest of any Native American on Alcatraz.

In July 1884, the captured Chiricachua Apache chief Ka-e-te-na, a compatriot of Geronimo, arrived on Alcatraz where he would spend nearly two years. Wrote Gen. George Crook upon the chief's release and return to the Arizona Territory: "His stay at Alcatraz has worked a complete reformation in his character." Crook's idea of reformation is open to interpretation.

Perhaps the most intriguing Indian captives were nineteen Hopi who arrived on Alcatraz in January of 1895. The orders stipulated they were to be confined at hard labor "until they shall evince … a desire to cease interference with the plans of the government for the civilization and education of its Indian wards, and will make proper promises of good behavior in the future." Part of the Hopis' incarceration included field trips to San Francisco — under guard — for the purpose of visiting public schools.

LIFE *During* PEACETIME

Army life on Alcatraz involved more than just maintaining unfinished fortifications and guarding military prisoners. Life continued normally at the post for the garrison whose duty was to defend the harbor. Troops came and went, commanding officers were transferred, births and deaths occurred.

Time went by, and the barren island began to take on a more civilized appearance. Enlisted men moved out of the tents and temporary barracks they had inhabited since the Civil War and into a spectacularly ugly wooden building atop the unfinished casemates behind the dock. Several duplex cottages were built north of the Citadel for the fort's sergeants, the backbone of any army installation.

Amenities made life more pleasant, and within a few years the fort boasted luxuries such as trees and gardens, a commissary, bowling alleys, a gymnasium, and a schoolhouse for the enlisted men. The little army steamer *General McPherson* made frequent trips between the Alcatraz, Angel Island and San Francisco, including a special "theater run" on Tuesday evenings.

In 1879, the Departmental Quartermaster of the Department of the Pacific carried out an inspection of the fort during a campaign to upgrade officer housing. In his report, the inspector made the first recorded mention of a popular nickname for the island: "Having inspected the 'Rock,' as it is called, in person," he observed a great need for improved quarters. "The 'Citadel' so

The dock area, showing the awkwardly built wooden barracks above the unfinished Bomb Proof Barracks. The area today has a more substantial structure built atop the old casemates. Note that the iron "throat" linings from the cannon embrasures have been removed — see Area #A in the Walking Tour on page 152.

called, into which each family is now crammed, without regard to health or even decency, is utterly unfit for use as a habitation by any persons not undergoing penal servitude."

He concluded his remarks with an unsettling recommendation: why not remove the prison and abandon Alcatraz? The departmental commander rejected this idea, but it was notable as being the first of many proposals over the next eighty years calling for the elimination of the island prison.

At least the Quartermaster's report resulted in improvements to living conditions for the island's officers. In 1880 the army erected three spacious Victorian homes for the senior staff on the slopes below the Citadel, the center residence reserved for the Commanding Officer. The interior of the Citadel was remodeled into six sets of junior officer's quarters, each with its own private entranceway spanning the now-defunct moat, and servants' quarters in the basement.

In 1885, the *Daily Alta California* sent a reporter to Alcatraz to write a story on the prison, but he also recorded a rather bucolic existence in the middle of the Bay:

"The buildings are chiefly clustered on the eastern slope of the island where they are protected from the ocean winds. Higher up, chicken houses and cow yards are seen, swelling the complement of domestic animals on the island. Along the roadside, as it nears the summit, are a succession of charming gothic cottages, occupied by the commanding officers (sic) of the garrison and their families, each with a little garden plot, and the voices of merry children make the air musical. On the summit proper, no implements of warfare ... except the solid shot, 15 inches in diameter, which ... cheerfully contribute to the adornment of the place, ranged in decorous rows, one above the other, around a tennis court, shielded from the still ocean breeze by a high wall, and lying in close proximity to a dainty garden, rich in fragrance and bloom."

Troops on Alcatraz followed a strictly dictated routine similar to that of army posts around the country. An unending succession of bugle calls and drum rolls marked the passage of each long day. The soldiers carried out a variety of daily exercises, alternating between marching drills, artillery practice, maintenance work, dress parades and Sunday inspections.

Non-military pastimes for the garrison included concerts presented by the fort's band and recreational facilities in the gymnasium, library and bowling alley. Island officers sponsored popular dress balls and "informal matinee hops." Guests from San Francisco and other army posts were frequent visitors to these fashionable social events.

Insights into daily life on the Rock appeared in reports of the post surgeon, who kept track of the myriad ailments and injuries that came across his threshold. One of the most common soldier

82

complaints was bruised and broken feet caused by untimely collisions with gun carriages and cannonballs.

Other minor injuries resulted from occupational hazards of the 19th century army: a contusion from being kicked by a mule; abrasions from falling down a staircase; a scalding in the kitchen; an eye punctured during bayonet practice; and a sprained back received while trying to escape.

Soldiers frequently reported to sick call exhibiting symptoms of alcoholism and gonorrhea, usually aggravated by visits to the flesh-pots of the Barbary Coast. Occasional cases of poison oak turned up, contracted during work details on the mainland and Angel Island. One soldier reported to the surgeon with an abrasion to his upper lip, caused by blowing a bugle.

Deaths also occurred on Alcatraz, the leading cause being disease. One accidental death occurred when a soldier fell off the unfinished casemates outside the enlisted barracks, landing on the dock below.

Sometimes violence was the source. Guards shot and killed at least three prisoners during escape attempts. On one occasion, a sergeant threw a soldier from a barracks window during a fight, fatally injuring the enlisted man who landed on an iron grating three stories below; the sergeant immediately killed himself with a revolver. The post dead, from both the prison and the regular garrison, were routinely buried in the cemetery on Angel Island.

In 1891, the fortress community was shaken when the young post surgeon, Capt. William Dietz, as well as his wife, were found dead in their quarters. The terse medical report read: *Mrs. Dietz came to her death at the hands of the Captain. Weapon used — shot gun, Caliber 10, subsequently the Captain killed himself with the same weapon. Insanity is supposed to be the cause of the tragedy.*

NEW DEFENSIVE PLANS

The old brick-and-earth gun batteries may have been obsolescent, but the army still considered Alcatraz critical for defending San Francisco. In May 1883, now-Colonel Mendell was informed he was being forwarded a shipment of new "submarine torpedoes" for storage on the island. Today these weapons would be recognized as electrically controlled underwater mines, but in the 1880s they were the latest word in military technology.

The Ordnance Department finished extensive tests of the mines, and the War Department sent 451 of the devices to San Francisco for storage until they could be planted in their mine fields. Washington decided that the only available space to warehouse the mines was in the casemates of the unfinished Bomb Proof Barracks.

The island's commander was aghast. The idea of stockpiling

Officer country in 1893, with the commander's house in the center. Though these structures have vanished, the stairway remains — see Area #K in the Walking Tour on page 155.

several hundred explosive devices was out of the question — especially considering that they would be located beneath the enlisted men's barracks. He relented when it was pointed out that the mines wouldn't actually be *filled* with TNT while stored in the casemates.

Col. Mendell dutifully remodeled part of the old casemates for the mines, but storage conditions turned out to be less than ideal: the rooms were dank and poorly ventilated, and the empty steel mines soon rusted on their wooden racks. Within a few months, Mendell had to assign a soldier and several prisoners to the full-time jobs of scraping and repainting. Plans were soon approved for constructing a spacious storehouse on Yerba Buena Island, and the mines were eventually moved to drier quarters.

Even after the engineers removed the mines in 1891, the casemates continued as part of the minefield system. Defense plans called for the construction of control rooms known as "mine casemates." Inside these rooms would be racks of electrical storage batteries, switchboard panels, and a terminus for cable lines connected to mines in the harbor. Once the mines were planted — in two huge mine fields, one on either side of Alcatraz — soldiers in the operating stations

84   *THE* ROCK

could detonate the mines either individually or in groups.

It was decided to convert the unused powder magazine at the north end of the casemates into one of the planned operating casemates, and Mendell spent $1,000 carrying out modifications. Aside from equipment and furnishings, the only major alteration he reported was digging a 100-foot-long cable tunnel leading out to the water's edge. After all Mendell's work, though, the mine casemate was apparently never used, or even tested.

An 1891 report on the status of fort ordnance recorded only seven cannon ready for service on Alcatraz — five 15-inch Rodmans and two old smoothbores that had been converted into rifles for target practice. In 1893 two more 15-inchers were mounted, making a grand total of nine cannon, all obsolete. No grander array of guns would ever again be emplaced on the island.

The army announced plans to redesign Alcatraz once again for modernized fortifications. After procrastinating since the Civil War, Congress began to release funds for a new generation of American harbor fortifications. The army, striking while the funds were available, recommended emplacing more than 200 huge, high-powered rifles and mortars for the defense of San Francisco.

This time the engineers proposed putting only five guns on Alcatraz, but they would be immense 12-inch rifles weighing over 50 tons each. Each gun and carriage was to sit atop a "gun lift" carriage operating along the lines of an enormous barber chair. In theory, the weapons would rise out of the ground on hydraulic platforms for each shot, and then lower into reinforced subterranean chambers for reloading. The five guns would be mounted in two extensive earth and concrete batteries, each several levels deep and three times the size of the entire Citadel.

By 1893, the Citadel was obsolete as a defensive work, its interior partitioned into apartments for junior officers. Note the carefully tended lawn surrounding the tennis court, and the decorative edging made of cannonballs.

The army quietly dropped its proposal for the grandiose gun lifts in 1897 (the only prototype never did work right), and instead suggested mounting Alcatraz's 12-inch guns on tried-and-true disappearing-style carriages. Wiser military minds, however, realized guns of this large caliber mounted so far inside the bay would have minimal strategic value. New plans were drawn up for smaller caliber, 6-inch guns whose role would be the protection of the minefields in front of the island.

In time, the army's enthusiasm for mounting modern guns on Alcatraz waned. No weapons were ever installed on the island under the massive fortification program, but the grandiose engineer drawings remain. The plans reveal that if the 12-inch guns had been emplaced on the island, the laboriously excavated parade ground would have been filled in again to provide earthen protection for one of the two batteries.

SPANISH-AMERICAN WAR AND BEYOND

America's ambassador to England called it "a splendid little war" and it lasted barely eight months. The Spanish-American War was a lopsided contest from the start, but the conflict didn't end when Spain surrendered. Filipinos were not eager to exchange domination by a European power for domination by an American power. A protracted insurrection broke out almost immediately against the U.S. occupiers. Bloody guerilla warfare between the U.S. Army and Filipino insurrectos continued for several years. Now known as the Philippine-American War, this horrific little war foreshadowed America's future entanglement in Vietnam.

The immediate effect on Alcatraz was a massive turnover in personnel. Army units arrived in San Francisco and sailed out again, first to fight against Spain and then against the Filipinos. Between 1898 and 1900 the post had no fewer than 13 different commanders. The Ordnance Department stripped the island of what little was left in the way of modern-weapon supplies when the remaining stores were shipped to the Philippines and Cuba.

Soon, soldiers started to return from overseas, many suffering from contagious tropical diseases. A large extension wing was added

More pleasant housing for the soldiers, this time the NCOs, with gingerbread trim under the eaves, laundry on the line and the ubiquitous cannonballs providing decoration.

to the fort's hospital for convalescing patients. The army also began to return shipments of soldiers who had been convicted of military offenses, with immediate and dramatic impact on the island.

During the summer of 1899, the Alcatraz prison population averaged 25 men; ten months later it had jumped to 441 and the island's garrison was doubled in size to handle the load. Every prison facility on Alcatraz seemed bursting at the seams. Something would have to give. More prison space was needed, and soon.

Many officers suggested that a modern prison facility was needed for the West, and Alcatraz was the obvious location. All pretense of harbor defense should be dropped, and the island remodeled for purely penal purposes. But departmental commander Maj. Gen. Arthur MacArthur had other feelings. He strongly believed that if a permanent military prison was established on the island, it *"would materially interfere with the Artillery defenses, which I hope some day may be installed there-on ... All of Alcatraz should be devoted to fortifications ... The island shall be dedicated exclusively and for all time to the purposes of defense."*

That wasn't to be. Alcatraz ceased to be a fortress only seven years later.

The steep slopes of Alcatraz gave rise to a precipitous form of architecture unique to the island. Here, the hospital rides high, supports masked by complex decorative latticework and surrounded by newly introduced ground cover.

CHANGING DUTY

How long had the old kerosene lantern been hanging from its iron bracket — maybe 20 years? Shortly after midnight on Jan. 6, 1902, it finally melted through its soldered connector link and fell 20 feet, shattering on the wooden floor of the cellblock. There was an instantaneous burst of greasy, yellow-white flame. The fire spread up the walls below the manually operated bar locking the cell doors.

The guard on duty in the cellblock grabbed a fire bucket and tossed water on the flames, extinguishing them immediately. But the screaming of men locked in wooden cells continued. Weeks later, the post's quartermaster reported: *"The prisoners are crazed with fear every time any unusual outside noise is made at night, fearing fire and that they will be burned to death. When, a few nights ago, the guard fired upon two escapes [sic], the prisoners in these prisons, believing it to be the fire alarm, shook their cell doors shrieking to be let out and not allowed to perish."*

The old prison was not the only firetrap on Alcatraz. Over the years, a maze of wooden-frame buildings had been erected atop the old fortifications. A 1901 map showed more than 50 structures scattered about the post. Every level area of real estate on the island seemed to sprout either a prison-related building or a support facility for the fortress. Cellblocks, officers' quarters, stables, barracks and warehouses stood everywhere. The only structures considered fire-proof were the old Citadel, the lighthouse, the original guardhouse and its ancient brick prison wing.

The size of the prison population had doubled since the Spanish-American War had ended. In January 1900, nearly 150 military convicts were crowded into the wooden prison when word arrived that 135 more prisoners were en route from Manila. The rotund commanding general of the Department of the Pacific, Maj. Gen. William "Pecos Bill" Shafter, hurriedly notified the War Department that this number would outstrip the intended capacity of Alcatraz by a factor of three.

He needed additional construction funds, and quickly.

Shafter got his requested funding almost immediately, and by

Prisoners at work breaking rocks, big ones into little ones, all day long. Eventually, their work would reshape Alcatraz.

February carpenters were constructing a second prison at the south end of the island. Located on engineer Mendell's parade ground, it was ready for occupancy within two months. The compound consisted of three wooden cellhouses, each containing two tiers of cells. A new guardhouse and latrine completed the facilities. The entire prison was surrounded by a 12-foot palisade wall and sentry walk. The "Upper Prison," as it came to be known, resembled a collection of wooden warehouses surrounded by a frontier stockade.

A 1902 report on the prison population documented 461 convicts on the Rock. At this time the prison was receiving men at the rate of more than 500 a year, but discharging nearly an identical number. Turnover was high because most prisoners were incarcerated for minor infractions. The report stated only three men were serving life sentences, while another one had 21 years left to serve. The rest of the population had sentences of two years or less.

Partly as a result of the near-catastrophic lantern fire, the army began a concentrated campaign in 1902 to improve military prison conditions. One contingent strongly argued an entirely new facility should be built on Angel Island. Alcatraz supporters, however, insisted the Rock was still suitable as a prison site so long as new construction didn't interfere with the new 6-inch batteries the War Department still planned for the island.

The wooden labyrinth of the Lower Prison. Halfway up the far wall, marked "B," is the brass oil lantern which fell, nearly turning the cellhouse into a crematorium.

Post Quartermaster Capt. A. M. Fuller had the unenviable responsibility of maintaining the claptrap assemblage of buildings on Alcatraz. Attempting to get matters off dead center, Fuller prepared a lengthy, photo-illustrated report in 1902 documenting facilities on the Rock.

The picture was grim. The old cell blocks of Lower Prison were "rotten and unsafe; the sanitary condition very dangoruos [sic] to health. They are dark and damp, and are fire traps of the most approved kind." The mess hall: "an absolute apology" and too far away from the new prison on the parade ground.

Upper Prison itself was far from ideal: *"Here are confined life, 40, 20, 15 year and lesser term men. All must be taken, three times a day and marched 1/4 mile, through the post, to meals, requiring 16 sentinels. This is a dangerous method, especially in winter, when darkness comes early and daylight comes late. Prisoners have escaped from these marching columns."*

Eventually, pro-Alcatraz forces prevailed, and approval was granted for expanding the Upper Prison. In 1904 work crews extended the stockade wall until it enclosed nearly the entire parade ground. A new mess hall, kitchen, shops, library and washhouse were built inside the expanded enclosure. When the project was completed, the entire convict population moved into Upper Prison. Lower Prison now became a laundry and workshops for the prisoners. With its new capacity of 307 inmates, the Rock was considered adequate for the Department of the Pacific's future penal needs.

Punishment for the convicts could still be severe in the early 20th century, though branding and flogging had long been outlawed. The old dungeons in the guardhouse had not been used for some years; instead, an iron cage had been erected in one of the cellhouses for the solitary confinement of troublesome inmates.

The *San Francisco Chronicle* reported on one such incorrigible prisoner. George Bender had been sent to Alcatraz for torching the homes of several Filipinos while stationed in Manila. He continued this habit after reaching the island, setting a fire in the prison. When the reporter saw him, Bender was carrying a ball-and-chain. The guards showed the journalist Bender's cell where a message had been scorched into the ceiling: "Bender the Firebug will burn this jail tonight." The army sent him to Kansas State Penitentiary before he could carry out this promise.

Between Bender the Firebug and crashing kerosene lanterns, the army determined that new, non-combustible facilities were needed on Alcatraz. The Quartermaster Department began by modernizing

Time has taken its toll on this image, but the details of a cellhouse in Upper Prison can still be made out. Unlike Lower Prison, these cells were only two tiers high, and double blocks flanked the mandatory potbellied stove.

FORTRESS ALCATRAZ

LITTLE ONES *FROM* BIG ONES

Alcatraz provided a ready labor pool for army posts all around the bay. At the time of the judge advocate's report in 1905, there were 271 men incarcerated on Alcatraz. He detailed the types of work military prisoners were engaged in at the time:

* At the Quartermaster Department, 105 prisoners worked on construction projects such as the new Alcatraz barracks and excavating in the quarry on Angel Island.

* Army engineers used 54 prisoners at Fort Barry in Marin County, constructing a rifle range.

* Thirty-six worked in the prison as cooks, waiters, orderlies, barbers, tailors, etc.

* Thirty-two were assigned to various clean-up, maintenance and "police" duties at harbor posts.

* Another 15 were listed on the sick rolls, either in the hospital, assigned to light duty, or confined to quarters.

* Six were third-class prisoners, and not assigned work.

* Another six awaited trial, probably confined to their cells.

* And one prisoner awaited release.

the garrison's quarters, and in 1905 drew up plans for a four-company barracks located atop the old Bomb Proof casemates. Following a now-established Alcatraz tradition, convict laborers would perform the majority of the work.

The quartermasters decided on a novel construction technique. Rather than use brick or reinforced concrete for the walls, pre-cast

concrete blocks were constructed on the dock, then hoisted into place atop the casemates.

Set in position and carefully pointed with cement, the giant building blocks gave a realistic-looking stone appearance. The hollow spaces inside the blocks also provided a convenient utility chase for locating dozens of ventilators and chimney flues.

Convict labor crews built the barracks in two sections; the island's enlisted men continuing to occupy their old wooden quarters until the new building was completed. When the northern half of the concrete structure was finally finished in early 1906, the architecturally abysmal 1870s barracks was demolished and the troops moved into "Building No. 64."

The completed structure contained room for nearly 300 soldiers, including NCO quarters and recreation rooms. Bachelor officers quarters and an officers club were located in the southern dog-leg of the building, while the old casemates in the basement now served as kitchens, mess halls, latrines and a post exchange. Due to extensive use of prison labor, the entire building had cost only $20,000.

The finished structure was so impressive, and the construction technique so efficient, that the army briefly considered going into business mass-producing the hollow concrete blocks for other government agencies.

Many visitors to Alcatraz over the years have been fooled by the sculpted walls of Building 64, and even today it's often described as being constructed of massive blocks of rough-hewn granite.

The quartermasters and convicts did their work well.

Military convicts at work building a new wash house for Upper Prison.

A NEW PRISON

In 1905, a judge advocate general visited the Rock and made some observations on general operations of the prison and the condition of the inmates:

"The prison rules are strict; obedience is rigidly enforced; no partiality is shown and the prisoners are taught that their future largely depends upon a faithful and conscientious observance of the prison rules ... Most violations of prison rules are met by reductions in grade, or by the deductions from good conduct time. No solitary confinement on bread and water diet has been imposed for a year or more ..."

Noon count at Upper Prison, 1903. The convicts are clothed in a fascinating array of cast-off uniforms dating back to the Indian Wars. In the earthy lexicon of the prison, this line-up procedure was referred to as "nuts to butts."

In a revealing comment, he made reference to two problems rarely discussed in formal records — homosexuality and drug abuse:

"The moral condition of the prisoners is better than was to be expected ... Obscene practices are of rare occurrence and are severely punished. But two prisoners are known to be addicted to the use of opium; one being a pronounced case."

In 1907 the War Department made a final decision regarding the future of Alcatraz. No longer would the island be designated as a harbor-defense fort; the army dropped the long-planned island batteries from the bay defense plans. The island was removed entirely from the control of the Department of the Pacific. The Rock would be the site of an enlarged, permanent prison designed to serve the entire United States Army west of the Rockies.

Walking the walls of the stockade yard, a never-ending duty for infantrymen assigned to guard military prisoners. The large, peak-roofed structure in the background was the new guard house.

On March 21st, the War Department officially designated the post "Pacific Branch, U.S. Military Prison, Alcatraz Island," a part of the long-established army prison at Ft. Leavenworth, Kansas. The infantry soldiers who had long (and reluctantly) served as guards were replaced by two companies of a newly formed U.S. Military Prison Guard.

The first commandant of the Military Prison was Maj. Reuben B. Turner, Quartermaster Corps. Promoted to lieutenant colonel, Turner buckled down to business; the War Department had appointed the major to his command because of his abilities as a construction engineer and provided him with $250,000 to build a prison representing the state of the art in penology.

Alcatraz at this time retained much of its 19th-century appearance. Dozens of temporary buildings still dotted the island, and the post had the look of a pleasant but unplanned western mountain village. Even though Lower Prison was no longer in use, its old cellblocks continued to be used for workspaces for the prisoners. Heat was provided by innumerable stoves and fireplaces, and the only light came from hundreds of kerosene lanterns. Few buildings had interior plumbing or running water.

By contrast, Turner's new Alcatraz would not only feature a

modern prison but centralized work facilities for the convicts and an updated utility system for the entire island. Wood frame residences and support buildings would be replaced by concrete structures of a harmonious architectural style. Before the end of summer, the commandant had turned in his first drawings for a modernized island.

Turner didn't design his prison in a vacuum. His plans had to be approved by the War Department, and for many months blueprints shuttled back and forth between Washington and Alcatraz.

To make space for his "New Prison," Turner put convicts to work leveling the island's north peak and demolishing the historic Citadel. The 50-year-old building stood exactly where the concrete cellhouse was planned, and before the close of 1908 prisoners were chipping it away from the west end to the east end.

Work on the new prison was well advanced by late 1909. The Citadel and other structures had been demolished, concrete foundations completed, and ironwork set up to support water tanks planned for the roof. Two old earthwork batteries had been filled in to create a level plateau on the west side of the cellhouse for a stockade exercise yard. The prison walls were starting to rise, and nearly a third of the cells were complete. Barges brought tons of iron bars for cell fronts, gates and window gratings to the island dock.

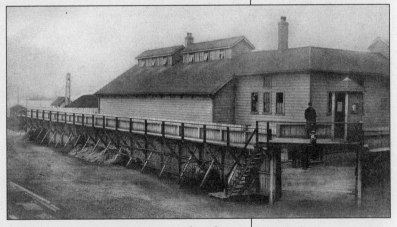

Turner was proud of the building: *"It will have accommodations for six hundred (600) military convicts (one to a cell), heated by steam, lighted by electricity, ventilated by a modified system of forced ventilation, with a steam cooking apparatus installed in the kitchen."*

The officer prepared monthly reports as work progressed, pointing out such construction details as installation of tamper-proof sinks and toilets, completion of skylights in the ceiling, testing the steam radiators, and a description of the steel cots provided in each cell — possibly the first time in Alcatraz history that prisoners did not have to sleep on pallets on the floor.

Turner realized the walls of New Prison would soon rise higher than the 1854 lighthouse still located atop the island. Plans were drawn up to construct a light tower atop the cellhouse roof, but the Lighthouse Board decided to build an entirely new tower, complete with attached keepers' quarters for three families. By late 1909 the new lighthouse stood complete, designed in the then-popular Mission Revival style that would complement the architecture of the various army buildings Turner planned for the island's new look.

Upper Prison, surrounded by wooden stockade walls like a western frontier fort, pictured on a foggy San Francisco afternoon. The entry gate to the compound is at lower right.

The island dock, 1902 and 1990. It is still the primary way on and off Alcatraz — see Area #A in the Walking Tour on page 152.

While the walls of New Prison were being erected, other convict work crews constructed a modern power plant and adjacent shop building at the northeast corner of Alcatraz. The new powerhouse was located directly atop the unfinished earthwork gun emplacements of Maj. Mendell's old Rodman batteries, and the foundations rested on the even earlier scarp walls of Lt. Tower's 1857 North Battery. The powerhouse contained boilers and generators to provide the entire island with both steam heat and electricity. One set of pumps furnished salt water for fire fighting and flushing, while another set lifted fresh water from transports at the dock to cisterns atop the prison. (Despite periodic drilling attempts, the army never located a source of fresh water on Alcatraz. Water came from the mainland, just as it does today.)

As work continued on new buildings, Alcatraz began to take on a silhouette very different from the one San Franciscans had known for the previous 60 years. The island lost its rounded, hilly form and the outline was replaced by the squared corners and high walls of the cellhouse and exercise yard. The powerhouse smokestack and lighthouse tower gave the appearance of a ship's masts flanking the

98   CHANGING DUTY

One fine spring morning, the newly completed Alcatraz barracks — and the entire island — had their structural stability sorely tested in what history has titled The Great Earthquake. The entry in the 1906 annual report was concise: "At about 5:30 on the morning of (April) 18th, a very severe earthquake shock occurred shaking all buildings, cracking many walls, and wrecking many chimneys." Soldiers living in the Building 64 barracks made a simultaneous dash for the only stairway, causing momentary panic and an impressive human traffic jam. A hurried inspection revealed Alcatraz had suffered relatively minor damage

THE GREAT EARTHQUAKE

— mostly broken chimneys and some cracked plumbing.

San Francisco had not been so lucky. Water mains and cisterns had ruptured throughout the city and fires burned out of control, fueled by broken gas mains under a hundred twisted streets. By late morning several fires had joined into one long front, eating away at the downtown financial district. Alcatraz troops were ferried in to assist in evacuating citizens, dynamiting fire breaks, and protecting abandoned buildings from looters.

By morning of April 19th, a firestorm approached the city's municipal jail on Broadway Street. Guards could hear an unearthly roar as oxygen rushed towards the flames. Buildings exploded in the superheated air and asphalt on the streets burst into flames as temperatures soared. The jailers decided it was time to evacuate their charges.

Talking some National Guardsmen and sailors into assisting them, the guards removed 176 prisoners from their cells, herded them through the blazing streets, and made their way to the emergency headquarters at Fort Mason.

Later in the afternoon the city's prisoners embarked on a heavily guarded launch headed for Alcatraz. When they pulled up alongside the island dock, the commanding officer had no option but to let the motley crew land. Space was found for the new arrivals in the already crowded cellblocks, and for the next nine days the Rock's military prisoners were joined by an eclectic mixture of muggers, thieves, junkies and drunken revelers — refugees from the Barbary Coast.

The leeward face of
Alcatraz, just prior to the
construction of New
Prison. From left, the old
cellblocks of Lower
Prison and Officers' Row
and above them, the
Citadel and the hospital.

"superstructure" of the main prison building. To some, the Rock now looked in profile very much like a battleship, lacking only gun turrets to make the illusion complete.

The prison complex was physically complete in late 1911, and on Feb. 6, 1912, many of the convicts who had worked in the construction gangs had the uncertain honor of becoming first occupants of the new cellhouse.

Alcatraz seemed ready to continue indefinitely in its role of incarcerating military prisoners. But no sooner were the buildings finished than another movement gained force to get the prison off the island. The Army Judge Advocate General, Maj. Gen. Enoch Crowder, went to the heart of the problem in 1913:

"[Alcatraz] lies directly in the path of commerce, and, surmounted as it is with the rather conspicuous new prison building is perhaps more prominent in the view of the incoming passenger and more the subject of his inquiry and that of residents and visitors generally than any other object in the harbor ... The buildings on Alcatraz constitute model detention barracks, and the sole objection to continuing it as such is ... the sentimental one that its prominence in the harbor advertises, in a way unfair to the military service, the discipline of the Army ..."

In modern terms, Alcatraz was bad for public relations.

High-ranking officers in the War Department proposed once again to close the prison, but this time they wanted to swap government property with another agency. The Bureau of Immigration expected a flood of European immigrants to arrive in California once the Panama Canal was finished, and the immigration people were

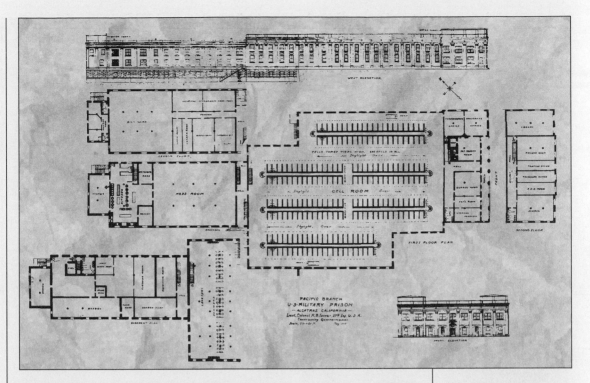

interested in using Alcatraz as an Ellis Island-type facility. And Gen. Crowder thought he had found a much better location for the military prison: the old masonry fort at Fort Point.

Two bills were introduced in Congress directing the transfer of Alcatraz and the establishment of a "detention barracks" at Fort Point. Late in 1913, convicts from Alcatraz were briefly assigned to Fort Point and began converting the abandoned fortification into a military prison. They enclosed the empty gun casemates with wooden partitions to serve as cell rooms, installed plumbing and latrines, and enlarged and remodeled the fort's powder magazines for guards' barracks.

How the military could have seriously considered moving the prisoners from the recently completed, modern cellhouse on Alcatraz into the drafty brick corridors of Fort Point is mystifying. Byzantine negotiations must have taken place between the War Department and the Bureau of Immigration to even consider the move, let alone commit money to carry it out. Congress, however, had the final word. Neither bill ever left committee, and the legislators refused to allocate funds either to finish the conversion work at Fort Point or to remodel the Alcatraz prison into a vast dormitory for immigrants.

The Rock belonged to the U.S. Army.

The final plan: Col. Turner's modernized Alcatraz cellhouse combined cell blocks, wash facilities, messhall, hospital and administration facilities in one gargantuan concrete building. The final structure matched this floor plan almost exactly.

PRISON

Construction of the new Alcatraz prison was a major undertaking by any standard, but — considering the isolated location in the middle of San Francisco Bay, the lack of fresh water for mixing concrete, and the unskilled labors of the convicts who carried out most of the work, — the project took on Herculean proportions. At the time of its completion in 1912 the prison was rumored to be the largest reinforced concrete structure in the world.

A great deal of site preparation took place before actual construction. Among other obsolete structures, the Citadel stood in the way of Maj. Turner's planned prison. It would have to go. The Citadel had originally been three stories high, with its first level surrounded by a dry moat. Most recently, the rooms on the lowest floor had served as kitchens and Chinese servants' quarters. Turner decided to leave this level of rooms intact, complete with the old dry ditch, to serve as a basement for the prison. Several of the numerous subterranean rooms would also provide excellent solitary-confinement space.

Perhaps as a cost-cutting move — or possibly out of nostalgia — Turner had several architectural details from the Citadel saved for reuse in the New Prison. The two ornate granite portals, which originally supported drawbridges spanning the moat, were dismantled for future use as entrances to the cellhouse, and cast-iron staircases and support beams from the demolished barracks were set aside for use in the interior. Brickbats from the demolished Citadel walls were mixed into the concrete work for the new building.

In 1909 the commandant received final permission to proceed with construction of the prison. A set of plans dated May 1910 revealed a penal facility that was immense compared to earlier complexes on the Rock. The entire prison would now be contained within a single, 500-foot long structure.

The main portion was the cellhouse proper, containing 600 one-man cells arranged in six, triple-tiered cellblocks. Each cellblock was designed as a freestanding structure within the outer walls of the cellhouse. Approximately a third of the cells were oriented facing the windows, while the rest of the cells faced other

A foreman surveys the debris of building a state-of-the-art prison. Iron girders in the background would soon support water cisterns atop the finished hospital wing.

The main cellhouse goes up, and it still stands today. See Area #M in the Walking Tour on pages 152 to 157.

tiers. Steam radiators along the exterior walls provided heat. Those fortunate enough to be assigned cells on an outside-facing block enjoyed both extra light and warmth. An administrative wing was located at the south end of the building, with office spaces for the commandant's staff, the guard contingent, a records room and library. In one corner of the administration wing was an isolated cell room for island's garrison prisoners; the army realized that the worst thing it could do to a guard undergoing punishment would be to put him in with the rest of the prisoners.

At the north end of the building a separate wing contained a hospital, kitchen, mess hall, barbershop and workrooms. Beneath the cellblocks were a spacious shower room and the underground hallways of the old Citadel. A "stockade" exercise yard surrounded by a 15-foot wall was attached to the cellhouse' western flank.

Army engineers supervising convict laborers once again directed the project, with civilian specialists brought in for more skilled jobs such as riveting and plastering. Unlike the earlier wooden cellhouses, the new prison was constructed entirely of reinforced concrete.

Riveted steel bar stock was used on all cell doors, replacing the strap iron used in the earlier prisons. The obsolete doors may have found another use, though; the grate cell fronts from Lower and Upper prisons appear to have been thrown into some concrete work to serve as reinforcing bars.

Iron girders above mark the location of the future Commandant's office, and are already overshadowing the now-doomed, original Alcatraz lighthouse. At left, convict workers in the area of the administration wing. In the background is a granite portal salvaged from the Citadel and re-erected as a doorway to the Commandant's office.

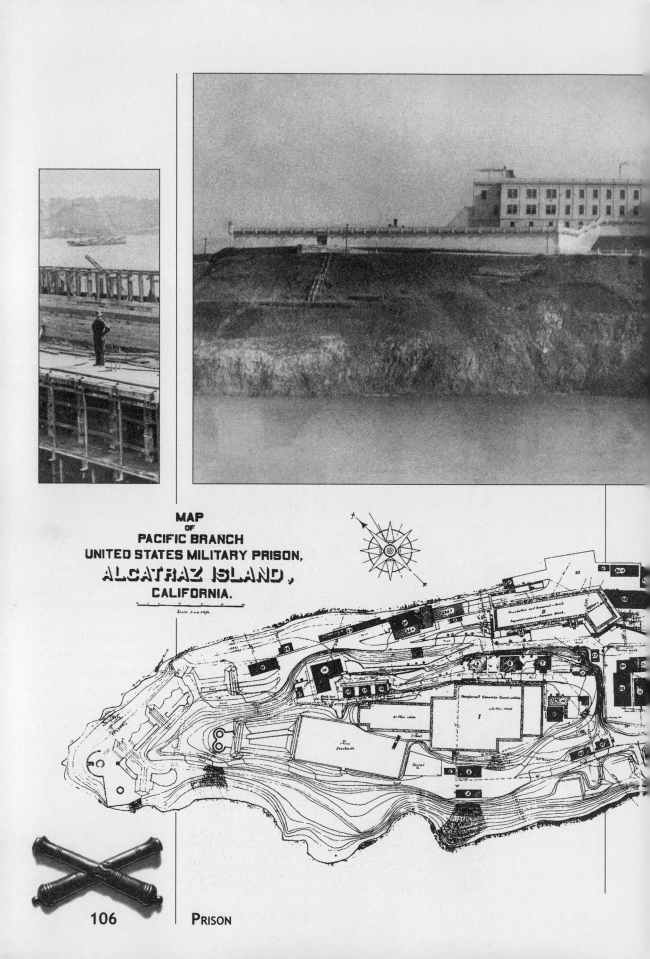

MAP
OF
PACIFIC BRANCH
UNITED STATES MILITARY PRISON,
ALCATRAZ ISLAND,
CALIFORNIA.

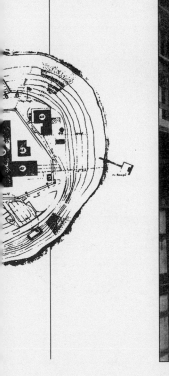

Above, the island has taken on its modern outline. The cellhouse, like a concrete Parthenon, spans the original location of Alcatraz' twin peaks.

Left, Mar. 20, 1911: The "New Prison" is nearing completion and in Block Six — later known as D-Block — only the concrete floor remains to be poured.

108

DISCIPLINARY BARRACKS

Pvt. Walter Stack was faced with a dilemma. Army life was definitely not turning out the way he had anticipated. He had already tried talking his way out of the army while in Plattsburgh Barracks in New York. Failing this, he had simply gone AWOL. Captured after a brief period of freedom, Stack had been shipped to the Philippines … and the Philippines were absolutely intoler-able. He wanted to go home to the States, and wondered what had ever possessed him to lie about his age and enlist at age 15 (a buddy had posed as his "guardian").

The solution to the problem had seemed simple; admit to falsifying his age and get booted out of the army. That certainly seemed better than spending the rest of his three-year hitch in Manila. His commanding officer hadn't seen it quite that way. Pvt. Stack was informed that even if he had enlisted falsely, he was now legally old enough to serve. There

was no simple way of discharging him. Stack's record wasn't great — there was that matter of deserting in Plattsburgh.

The teenage soldier was offered two unpleasant alternatives. He could serve out the remaining two years of his enlistment or spend nine months in the Disciplinary Barracks on Alcatraz, receiving a dishonorable discharge. Stack did the math and opted for the lesser sentence on the Rock. It was the worst choice he ever made.

Pvt. Stack was typical of military prisoners of the period; young, confused and in need of a disciplined regime. In 1925, the year Stack arrived on Alcatraz, the army prison had changed little physically from the time of its completion a dozen years earlier. But there had been notable advances in how it operated. The growing science of penology dictated that the goal of imprisonment was rehabilitation rather than punishment. On Alcatraz the first difference had been a title change in 1915 from "Pacific Branch, Military Prison" to "Pacific Branch, United States Disciplinary Barracks."

The great steel cages go into place: The area today is missing the spiral staircases providing access to the upper cell tiers, and ramps leading to the library and assembly hall in the administration wing — *see Area #M in the Walking Tour on page 155.*

The change had been more than semantic; the name signified a place of discipline and education rather than confinement. The inmates were now officially assigned to the 2nd Disciplinary Battalion, composed of the 5th, 6th, 7th and 8th Companies and the wonderfully named 2nd Disciplinary Band. In effect, the army considered the men to be soldiers assigned to punishment companies. Even the term "military convict" had been dropped.

Most prisoners underwent training while on Alcatraz and many were offered the option of being restored to full military duty. From the number of soldiers successfully sent back to the regular army ("returned to the colors" in the parlance of the day) or released to society, the idea seemed to work.

Newly arrived men were still categorized as "general prisoners" but the Disciplinary Barracks' system immediately appointed most of them to the rank of First Class. From this class came the men assigned to the Disciplinary Companies. These prisoners, referred to as "Disciples," enjoyed a fair degree of privileges as stipulated by War Department regulations.

The Disciples worked at regular jobs in the Barracks and received instruction in vocational skills useful upon discharge. Military science courses such as signaling, artillery, and field construction provided training to men who sought reinstatement as soldiers. The Barracks also offered night classes ranging from remedial education to University of California extension courses.

The Alcatraz Medical staff, 1918. The black soldier in the second row is Sgt. Stroud, a former prisoner who regained regular-soldier status and became an anesthetist in the prison hospital.

Then there were the soldiers already convicted of crimes and issued dishonorable discharges. These "numbered prisoners" served straight time at Alcatraz, and were discharged from the Barracks at the end of their sentences. These inmates did not rank the distinction of being known by name but were referred to only by their serial numbers. They suffered from a loss of personal identity and also reductions in privileges.

"Numbers" were quartered separately from the Disciplinary Companies and worked full-time without benefit of advanced training or earning good-time credits toward reduction of sentence. Numbered prisoners couldn't associate with the prisoners of the First Class or even converse with their fellow Numbers while at work.

Of course, things could still go downhill for prisoners after they arrived on Alcatraz. The only lower category of prisoners consisted of men undergoing punishment. This treatment ranged from being restricted to cells to full-bore solitary confinement in the dungeons below the cellhouse. Few men wanted to experience these lower levels of Alcatraz discipline. There, in the remains of the old Citadel, six rooms had been converted to isolation cells. Prisoners locked away there were frequently chained in a standing position to barred cell doors for eight-hour stretches. There were no lights, and meals could be reduced to the still-prescribed ration of bread and water.

Military law stated that a man couldn't be kept down there longer than 14 days at a stretch. It was usually enough.

When Pvt. Stack arrived on Alcatraz, he was immediately given a registry number, issued a black-dyed denim uniform and assigned a cell on the top tier of Block No. 2. His new surroundings were stark. The cell measured 5 by 9 feet, with a steel cot suspended by chains hanging from one wall and a tiny folding table and chair attached to the opposite wall. A metal sink with push-button faucet and a porcelain toilet with no toilet seat completed the furnishings. He faced across the aisle at an endless row of duplicate cells.

The walls were white and the bars a uniform dull black. Large mottos were stenciled on the walls of the cellhouse at various locations, intended to inspire prisoners toward moral improvement: THE STONE REJECTED BY THE BUILDER HAS BECOME THE TOP OF THE ARCH, HOPE SPRINGS ETERNAL, and THE OBJECTIVE OF LIFE IS TO ACHIEVE PERFECT CHARACTER. It was going to be a long nine months.

Being a new arrival sentenced to a Dishonorable, the army considered Stack a numbered prisoner, but to the rest of the population he was a "fish." You had to prove yourself first to the guard staff before you were given work, and then to the rest of the inmates before they considered you a "solid con" and accepted you into the prison's inside hierarchy. For a rebellious seventeen-year-old, it was not easy to adapt.

The quarry where prisoners preyed on each other, opposite, is today occupied by the penitentiary laundry and tailor shop — see Area #O in the Walking Tour on page 156.

Alcatraz' monthly periodical *The Rock* cheerfully portrayed the Disciplinary Barracks as a minimum security operation, where most cells served as places of confinement only at night and misguided men worked diligently at regaining their status as good soldiers and citizens; where the all-prisoner "White Sox" and "Colored Giants" baseball teams played sandlot ball in the stockade yard, and the Sunday evening sing-a-long sessions were filled to capacity; and where Disciples watched educational movies such as "Manufacture of the Stetson Hat," "Queer Fish and Shells," and the ever-popular "Gathering Cocoa."

A couple of passages from a 1919 army inspection of the Disciplinary Barracks give insight into the conflicting nature of the facility: *"The Commandant insists the Barracks shall NOT be called a prison"* and *"In providing suits for discharged men, care is taken to vary the patterns, so that men shall not go out with the brand of Alcatraz upon them."*

More than half a century later, Walt Stack remembered an island far different from the public-relations version — men stabbed while working in the quarry, a man tossed from the third-level tier during a fight, and an accidental encounter with a convict in the act of buggering a young prisoner, who told Walt he was a "dead stoolie" if he ever reported what he had seen.

THE WOLVES OF ALCATRAZ

For 17-year-old Walt Stack, Prisoner #15331, Alcatraz was a frightening, dangerous place. His first work assignment was in the rock quarry on the west side of the island, a rugged area notable for its remoteness from the rest of the prison and its secluded corners. It was the domain of hardened prisoners who preyed on younger and weaker "fish." Physical attacks and rapes occurred at startling intervals.

For Stack, memories of his two months on the rockpile stayed with him long after he left the Disciplinary Barracks. "I was the most terrorized there I ever felt in my life," he later recalled. "There were lots of wolves there. You know, older guys who would get their guns off on some young kid. They did it to some kids so much, they kind of turned them into women."

Military doctors during this period considered homosexuality as the result of cerebral lesions, in the same class as brain cancer. Whatever the reason, Stack was horrified by the buggery behind the rockpile. Only 17, he might have seemed easy pickings himself, but Stack was determined to be tough case. He vowed never to be dessert for the wolves, and also never to be a stoolie for the guards, even though they might have protected him.

Accordingly, he prepared for battle. "I stashed rocks all around the rockpile that I could use as weapons if they tried to grab me," said Stack. "And I put out the word: Stack will kill anyone trying to get into his pants. I meant it. I'd rather have gone to the electric chair than have some son-of-a-bitch turn me into a queer."

The remaining weeks were marked by constant fear. Stack worked at cutting and hauling rock, always staying within quick reach of his piles of ammunition, while also trying to watch everything simultaneously.

Unscathed, Stack graduated to relatively safer conditions in the prison laundry. "I don't give a shit any more [about my prison term]," said Stack in a 1990 interview. "I just want everyone to know what the Rock was really like."

Alcatraz by day — this 1914 view illustrates the massive cutaway of the parade ground, the new prison, the new lighthouse and, under construction, a breakwater to hold crushed rock thrown over the side.

The War Department may have lauded the Disciplinary Barracks as a model of rehabilitation, but the Rock was still a prison with all the inherent dangers.

UNCLE SAM's DEVIL'S ISLAND

The prison population during the 1920s averaged between 300 and 450 men. Occasionally, special prisoners still arrived on Alcatraz, such as a group of Quakers claiming conscientious objector status, and Franz Bopp, the German Consul General during the First World War, who was kept on the island during two lengthy trials for wartime offenses. On at least one occasion the population exceeded 550 prisoners, nearly filling the cellblocks to capacity.

Despite army attempts to improve the reputation of Alcatraz, its image as a secret bastille tunneled with moldering passageways continued to grow in popular mythology. Long off-limits to the public, the highly visible island in the middle of San Francisco Bay became a constant source of interest to civilians. Newspaper writers making periodic visits to the Disciplinary Barracks continued to speak of "Spanish dungeons" carved out of solid rock (in reality, the brick-lined solitary cells in the remains of the Citadel) and began making references to Alcatraz as "Uncle Sam's Devil's Island." Long before the arrival of such notorious later residents as Machine Gun Kelly and Doc Barker, the Rock had an ignoble public image.

One of the most popular misconceptions about Alcatraz was that it was escape-proof. True, the army had originally designated the island as a prison in 1861 because of the natural barriers it presented to fleeing convicts, but there had been escapes anyway.

Only a few escape attempts occurred from inside the army cellblocks, as most military convicts were assigned daily work duties around the island post. They simply awaited an opportune moment to slip away from their guards and find a way to float or swim to the mainland. In 1878, two prisoners managed to escape Alcatraz through the simple expedient of stealing a small boat and rowing to San Francisco.

In 1906, four prisoners made off with a large butter vat from the bakery and tried to paddle to the mainland. A combination of contrary winds and tides forced them back onto the island where they hid out for awhile in an abandoned powder magazine. Sentries eventually rounded them up and clapped them in irons.

The following year, three more men made a similarly unsuccessful yachting attempt in a bread-kneading trough (security must have been very lax in the bakery), and a lone con almost made it to the city by floating away on a log. He was hit by a passing ferryboat and hauled aboard for a return trip to the island.

Clinging to flotsam found along the shore was a popular escape ploy; two men constructed a raft out of driftwood in 1912, and two others shoved off on a log in 1916. Another pair of prisoners were found in the bay floating on a plank in 1927, while still two more were caught clinging to a discarded ladder in 1929.

Three especially inventive prisoners in 1930 pried loose a bar in a barbershop window, clambered to the water's edge and grabbed several planks they had hidden earlier. The cold waters of the bay quickly changed their minds, and they were found crying for help and drifting in the general direction of Berkeley.

A few men found ways to get off the island without even getting their feet wet. In 1903 four enterprising prisoners made up a set of

And by night — a realistic depiction of the prison by moonlight, from a postcard of the period. The view is unique in that it shows the barracks, Upper Prison, New Prison and the new lighthouse all standing at the same time.

YOU DAMN WEST POINTERS!

Most of the escapees didn't actually make their breaks from the island but instead waited until assignment to work details at other posts; getaways were much easier from the mainland. The year 1877 was especially notable, when no fewer than nine prisoners escaped from work assignments at Point San Jose.

A young officer recalled one such escape attempt in his memoirs. Recently graduated from the Military Academy, the new lieutenant was spending a summer-long furlough with his family in San Francisco. "A prisoner engaged in work at Fort Mason, where we lived, had escaped. He was a burly fellow armed with a scythe, and great consternation reigned in the post ... It was none of my business, but I had tracked trails too often with the Apaches not to pick up this one. His hiding place was easy to locate, and I had him covered before he had a chance to make a move. When I turned him over to the guard, he just spat at me and snarled, 'You damn West Pointers!'"

2nd Lt. Douglas MacArthur, Class of '03, had won his first engagement.

formal looking papers recommending their own release, forged the commander's signature, and mailed the documents to the War Department. Army bureaucrats duly processed the papers and returned the approved discharge orders to Alcatraz. The four were given a military escort to the mainland and set free. The ringleader, a noted forger, was tracked down a few days later while recovering from a celebratory binge in San Francisco.

The Great Influenza Epidemic of 1918 gave two inmates a unique escape opportunity. Donning flu masks and stolen officers' uniforms, they casually boarded an army launch headed for the Presidio, mingling en route with genuine officers commuting to the city. The pair was located several days later in Modesto, California, where they were arrested by the local sheriff and returned to the Rock.

In 1926, prison authorities got wind of a massive escape being planned by dozens of inmates. The convicts' logic was that if enough men tried to break out simultaneously, the guards couldn't stop them all and the odds were in favor of a majority reaching the mainland. Army lore has it that the commandant, Col. G. Maury Cralle, gathered the entire disciplinary population on the parade ground, pointed toward San Francisco, and invited them to try the swim. He guaranteed there would be no interference from his guards.

The prisoners reportedly took a long look at the surging current and white-capped swells, and sheepishly returned to the cellhouse.

The last recorded military prisoner attempting to escape Alcatraz may have accomplished his goal. Scorning all flotation devices, convict Jack Allen simply greased his body and plunged into the bay's waters one cold June night in 1930. He hasn't been seen since.

THE PRISON FAMILY LIFE

The island continued to be home to dozens of wives and children of the prison's garrison. At the time Private Stack was serving time in the Disciplinary Barracks, the families of the island's military and civilian employees were experiencing Alcatraz from a very different point of view.

Military convicts were such a common sight around the island that families and prisoners mingled freely with little friction. "Disciples" and "Numbers" were everywhere, working on the dock, gardening, pruning trees, painting buildings, constructing new seawalls, or simply walking freely between the cellhouse and the industrial buildings. Fear of being attacked by convicts was almost unknown, at least among the guards and their families. Violence in the Disciplinary Barracks was strictly a con-to-con confrontation.

On at least one occasion, an irate father chased away an exhibitionist prisoner from outside a bedroom window. Most prisoners, however, were highly trusted, and many worked as au pairs for families with children.

Many households were also provided with prisoners who worked as family servants or officer valets. A 1926 guidebook to

A baseball game in the exercise yard is interrupted by a fistfight. The guards on the stockade wall seem to be more interested in the outcome than many of the prisoners. Note that some convicts have joined the guards along the wall, and that the batting order is listed by prisoner number rather than by name.

U.S. Army posts referred to the Rock as *"A paradise for servants. Pass boys from the Disciplinary Barracks are eager to work for officers for small pay which is held in trust for them. The usual pay is a few packs of cigarettes ..."*

Mr. William Elliott, the civilian engineer who operated the powerhouse, was assigned several prisoners to assist with maintenance, along with the occasional soldier "volunteer" from the island garrison. The Elliott family was also assigned a pass man who served as a houseboy in their nearby residence. The family celebrated "Bill's" twenty-first birthday with a party in their home.

Life continued for the children much as it would have on any army post. There were special benefits to living on the Rock. There was a boat ride at 8:20 every morning to Fort Mason, where a government bus — complete with guard — shuttled them to school in San Francisco. There were hide-and-seek games among the abandoned fortifications. Alcatraz' steep sidewalks made for excellent roller skating, and after the convicts paved the roads with concrete the children attained blood-chilling speeds going down the switchback roadway. The hairpin turns only made life more interesting. And hand-held sails of canvas would propel a skating child most of the way around the island.

Family snapshots on Alcatraz tended to be unique. Two-year-old Kenneth Mickelwaite gets a between-innings hug from his buddy Mason, a prisoner in his baseball uniform. The "A" on the cap stood for "Alcatraz."

Kenneth's father, a company officer, served three years on the island.

Movies shown in the cellhouse were especially popular with children. The Catholic chaplain had contacts with film distributors in San Francisco, and during the 1920s first-run movies often found their way onto the Rock before debuting at movie palaces on Market Street. On Wednesday and Sunday nights, First Class prisoners would gather in the prison assembly room to watch the latest silent movies and talkies. Everyone on the island was welcome to these screenings, and children would settle by prisoners' feet in the front row. Their parents found chairs a discreet distance away.

An unusual aspect of an unusual island were the so-called "Alcatraz Fights" of the 1910s and '20s. The army staged these pugilistic events periodically on Friday nights, featuring boxing matches between inmates chosen from the Disciplinary Barracks' population. On fight nights, the army launches *General Coxe* and *Alcatraz* arrived at the island dock loaded with soldiers and officers from neighboring posts along with interested civilian guests who had finessed an invitation. The audience gathered around a makeshift boxing ring in the middle of the mess hall and sat through a program featuring as many as a dozen matches. Tradition has it that bouts were arranged between cons who had ongoing grudges, and the boxing at times approached barely restrained mayhem. The grand finale was a Battle Royale with several blindfolded boxers slugging it out simultaneously.

In the early 1930s the army once again reviewed its need for a military prison in San Francisco. Operating Alcatraz was a costly affair, and the military had felt a monetary pinch since the start of the Great Depression. The block-long sign reading U. S. DISCIPLINARY BARRACKS emblazoned across the stockade wall did little to increase the military's public-relations image with civilians. The citizens of San Francisco became increasingly unhappy with a major army prison in their view of the bay.

At the same time, the Department of Justice began casting about for a new maximum-security prison. There had been a huge increase in the population of the country's federal penitentiaries during the previous decade, partly resulting from crackdowns on organized

Army prisoners lined up for work details in the industrial area on the north end of the island. The guards are distinguished from prisoners by their campaign hats, while the fellow in the foreground seems to be undergoing some sort of punishment involving a stork-like stance and a shovel.

crime and bootleggers. Attorney General Homer Cummings and FBI Director J. Edgar Hoover wanted to establish a "super prison" to handle the most incorrigible and notorious prisoners from this mushrooming population.

Cummings and Hoover also wanted a highly visible facility that would serve as a perceptible deterrent. The new prison would also have to be strong enough to handle escape artists who had managed to wriggle and blast their ways out of existing federal penitentiaries such as Leavenworth, Atlanta and McNeill Island.

Alcatraz Island seemed to fit Justice Department needs in nearly every respect. If the citizens of San Francisco had been unhappy with a Disciplinary Barracks, they were now absolutely distraught at the prospect of an island full of bootlegging gangsters and mad-dog murderers. To Hoover and Cummings, though, civilian concerns were of little importance.

Negotiations with the Department of Justice for the transfer of Alcatraz began in May of 1933. The army had no objections to

A pass boy runs an errand along the parade ground below the impressive bulk of the Commandant's new residence. At the foot of the hillside is a fenced enclosure marking the island's childrens' playground.

releasing the island to another agency; not only would closing the Barracks save the War Department a handsome sum, it would also allow consolidation of its disciplinary activities at Fort Jay, New Jersey, and Fort Leavenworth, Kansas. The process moved quickly and on Oct.13, 1933, Secretary of War George Dern signed an initial five-year permit transferring Alcatraz to the Bureau of Prisons.

Much work needed to be done before Alcatraz could become the super prison of Director Hoover's imagination. The army never intended its facilities to be maximum security, and before the end of 1933 a major overhaul of the cellhouse and the entire island began. Riveted strap-steel cell fronts and window sashes were ripped out and replaced by tool-proof steel bars. Locks on cell doors were replaced by remote-control mechanisms that no lockpick artist could finesse. Guard towers sprouted around the perimeter of the island, and signs were put up warning boats to keep a distance of 200 yards or risk being fired upon.

Thousands of feet of barbed wire were strung around the island

The Commandant's residence in the '20s, then and now — see Area #L in the Walking Tour on page 155. Opposite, the entrance to Lower Prison — see Area #B in the Walking Tour on page 152.

to corral the prisoners and keep them a safe distance from the wives and children of the guards. The Bureau of Prisons looked with great concern upon the dozens of tunnels, powder magazines and underground storerooms left over from the old fortifications. Tons of concrete and steel were used to seal potential hiding places from escaping cons.

In early 1934 the army transferred most of its Alcatraz prisoners to Fort Jay, while granting some men reductions in sentence and early release. Not all the military inmates were scheduled to depart, though. The army arranged to leave behind their hardcore prisoners for the Department of Justice to manage.

Soldiers remaining on the Rock were an unsavory lot, serving sentences for crimes such as robbery, assault, rape and manslaughter. These men, the first residents of the new penitentiary, received numbers 1 through 32. Federal Prisoner #1 was Frank Bolt from Schofield Barracks, Hawaii, serving a 5-year sentence for sodomy.

New families also started to arrive on the island in early 1934. Handpicked Correctional Officers from Leavenworth and Atlanta traveled to Alcatraz to set up the operations for the new penitentiary, and familiar faces from the army era began to disappear. For the few remaining civilian employees staying on to operate island utilities, the changes were unwelcome. Gone were the close-knit military families and the pleasant routine of an army post, even one with a disciplinary barracks looming overhead. For some, Alcatraz no longer felt like home.

Soldiers were replaced by blue-clad officers of the Federal Bureau of Prisons. Security was raised to levels never before experienced on the Rock. Gates appeared all over the island in preparation for the "irredeemable types" scheduled to arrive, and restrictions on travel crimped social life. The "Justice people" even removed family telephones.

The first federal convicts arrived on Aug. 11, 1934. Brought down by train from McNeill Island, Washington, the fourteen men were locked in their cells before newspapers got wind of the transfer.

On August 22, another trainload was scheduled to reach Alcatraz and this time the media was awake. Extensive publicity surrounded the departure of 53 men from Atlanta Federal Penitentiary, and reporters had the railroad terminal at Oakland staked out. Staying a step ahead of the press, the prison authorities diverted the heavily guarded train and rerouted it through the little railroad town of Tiburon. There, the three-car train was rolled onto a barge and towed to Alcatraz. Not to be outdone, news reporters chartered boats of their own and dogged the barge and train all the way to the island. Staying just outside the 200-yard limit, they snapped pictures of prisoners being unloaded onto the dock by straw-hatted federal agents.

Once on the island, the guards shackled the convicts together into a single long chain and started them on a circuitous march up the perimeter road leading to the back entrance to the cellhouse. Guards armed with machine guns lined a route that led right past the upstairs windows of the powerhouse engineer.

The Elliott family — and the entire population of Alcatraz — had

been given strict orders not to leave their residences until the men were safely locked in their cells; no hostage situations were going to mar the penitentiary's opening day. But the rules didn't say anything about discreetly watching the passing parade of prisoners.

The families had a birds-eye view of the convict chain as it lock-stepped up the roadway. Children watched in fascination as the armed dock guards ran around the perimeter of the island and repositioned themselves along the road just before the marching prisoners came into view; the idea was apparently to give the cons an exaggerated impression of the size of the guard staff and its potential firepower. Civilians were shocked to see prisoners shackled hand and foot; despite decades on the island, many had never seen a prisoner in chains.

The family members carefully scrutinized the faces of the convicts as they shuffled up the road outside their window. They had a very good idea of who should be in that chain. The newspapers had been full of rumors since the prison train left Atlanta four days previously.

Teenager Mary Elliott, daughter of the power-house engineer, nudged her mother and pointed to a stocky man with a pronounced double chin, midway in the chain of prisoners. He had a scar gleaming on his cheek.

"There he is, Ma! That's Al Capone!"

The United States Penitentiary, Alcatraz Island, was ready for business. Eighty years of army presence on the Rock had ended.

THE ARMY RETURNS

THE ARMY RETURNS

The convicts milling around the exercise yard formed into a long, denim-clad line. The Sunday morning baseball game was over, and unbending penitentiary routine required that the men now return to their cells before going to the dining hall for lunch. The line began to move into the cellhouse, each inmate passing through a metal detector and proceeding to his cell to be locked in.

Correctional officers then walked the perimeter of each tier of cells, counting the men standing face-forward just inside the barred doors. This noontime head count was reported to the armory for verification. Once all the men were accounted for, approval was finally given to begin serving lunch. A bell sounded, and the men were let out of their cells to march silently toward the dining hall.

As the first cons passed through the barred door to the mess hall, though, the line began bunching up in front of a large blackboard. Hastily chalked on the board that usually posted baseball scores was a message: *At 7:55 a.m. Hawaiian Time, Japanese planes attacked and inflicted serious damage on United States military forces on the Island of Oahu …*

The warden himself had copied down one of the news bulletins as it was broadcast over the radio. Hurrying into the cellhouse, he had the text chalked onto the blackboard and placed where the convicts could read it.

Most inmates stood stunned as they absorbed the news. Shock, disbelief, and outrage were their first reactions. Felons they might be, but they were still patriots. But a twisted few celebrated at the announcement — self-styled anarchists and old-line Bolsheviks who thought an end was coming to the decadent, imperialistic America they hated, and some who smiled broadly simply because they were outcasts, finding joy in any misery that befell society.

Alcatraz Island had not been a formally recognized military fortification since 1907, despite the few aging army cannon still decorating the parade ground. The island, however, still commanded a tactically important location in the middle of San Francisco Bay. To Lt. Gen. John L. DeWitt at the Presidio, commander of the Fourth

The Alcatraz girl's club (nicknamed "JUGS" by its innocent members for "Just Us Girls") strikes a precarious pose atop an ancient Rodman left behind by the army as a decoration. Soon the old cannons would be ripped out and smelted down for scrap and replaced by modern antiaircraft guns, as the army once again realized Alcatraz' strategic location.

Several of the more patriotic inmates and long-time solid cons were assigned tasks such as this one — welding a seam on a submarine-net flotation buoy, one of several used to wall off the Golden Gate from enemy submarines.

U.S. Army and Western Defense Command, the Rock was still government property that could mount guns. But DeWitt was going to have problems with Alcatraz.

When San Francisco staged its first air-raid alert on the night of Dec. 9, 1941, the army considered the results less than successful. Lights twinkled all over the Bay Area. The Federal Penitentiary on Alcatraz sat fully illuminated in the middle of the bay, lighthouse flashing and cellhouse walls lit up by the glare of scores of floodlights. One guard remembered that the island "glowed like a Christmas tree." But Alcatraz was not the only twinkling landmark. The next day the *San Francisco Chronicle* reported "blacked-out San Francisco looked like New Orleans at Mardi Gras time."

DeWitt was furious. "I never saw such apathy … it was criminal, it was shameful," he raged. The general aimed some of his wrath directly at the Rock. If he couldn't get the civilian population to cooperate, he should at least be able to have another government facility set a good example.

The general tried complaining directly to Warden James A. Johnston on Alcatraz. The warden was a man who kept a tight rein over his operation, and no outsider told him what to do with his prison. His response to DeWitt was to the effect that 'Security is our business out here. The lights stay on.'

By one report, DeWitt then threatened to shoot out the island's lights if they weren't shut off voluntarily during the next blackout. Gen. DeWitt never let loose at Alcatraz, deciding he needed a higher authority to blow away the obstinate Johnston. A coded message was sent to the State, War and Navy Building in Washington, where the Secretary of War placed a phone call. 'It seems we a have a problem out in California …'

A memorandum allegedly was fired at Warden Johnston, signed by the Attorney General. Alcatraz, the warden was informed in blunt language, would comply with military blackout regulations completely. Johnston grumbled, but knew when he was licked. During the next air-raid alert, the island's lights were snuffed. Even the lighthouse went dark. Alcatraz officers continued to make their rounds, but now they were equipped with flashlights with special purple bulbs. DeWitt was satisfied.

The threat of aerial attack was firmly lodged in the mind of defensive tacticians — Japanese planes had already devastated Pearl Harbor and gone on to assault the Philippines, Hong Kong and Darwin, Australia. German bombs were raining down on London. San Francisco, with its many military installations and harbor facilities, was an obvious target. Temporary antiaircraft batteries were soon spouting from hilltops all over the Bay Area. Alcatraz, it was determined, was a perfect midbay counterpart to AA emplacements being dug around Marin County forts, on Angel Island, and atop the few undeveloped hills in San Francisco.

A few months into 1942, an Army Engineer work crew appeared on the island with orders to begin preparing mounts for four 40mm antiaircraft guns. Warden Johnston offered no resistance this time. Either he had seen the benefits of having the military on the island, or he had received another memorandum from Washington. Army personnel received the full support and assistance of Johnston's correctional staff.

The cellhouse was the most logical place on the island for the gun emplacements. With an elevation of 150 feet, its rooftop afforded a nearly unobstructed view of the harbor, and as long as the gunners were careful not to shoot at the water tank or the lighthouse, the field of fire covered much of the Bay.

In order to avoid clustering all the AA guns in one location, army planners decided to place only two weapons on the prison roof while the remaining pair would be mounted at opposite ends of the island, one on the roof of the apartment house known as "B-C Building" to island families and the other atop the Model Industries factory building. Carpenters erected two wooden platforms at the extreme corners of the cellhouse, another on top of the elevator house on the Model Industries, and the fourth atop of the "solarium" sunroom on the apartment house roof. Workers painted the platforms to match the cream-colored concrete walls of the buildings in an effort to camouflage them.

The battery was composed of four 40mm Bofors-type antiaircraft guns, mechanical range computers, some .50 caliber Browning

The Biggee Drayage Company does its bit for the war effort by hoisting a 40mm antiaircraft gun to the top of the guards' apartment house. The other three guns assigned to Alcatraz were placed atop the prison and industries buildings.

From the pages of a photo album kept by a Correctional Officer during the war, slices of life on The Rock. These two snapshots were titled "Inspection" and "The Gun."

machine guns for close-in defense, and shelters for crews and ammunition. The intense security of the federal penitentiary had to be respected, though. Access to the only flight of stairs leading to the roof of the cellhouse was through the front door of the administration wing — a maze of double-locked sallyport gates. Rather than make the soldiers go through this time-consuming security system en route to their guns, a special "security stairway" with a locked door was built against the east face of the prison building solely for their use. Tarpaper-covered "ready rooms" were built near each weapon for the GIs posted at each emplacement.

Once the contractors finished building the emplacements U.S. Army engineers from the Presidio arrived on the island to oversee the arrival and installation of the actual antiaircraft guns. Since the 40mm weapons were mobile artillery and came mounted on wheeled carriages, the engineers had the weapons loaded onto a cargo barge and towed to the island. The barges arrival was timed to correspond with high tide, and the trucks and guns rolled right onto the Alcatraz dock and up the switchback road to the cellhouse, apartment building and industries area. Heavy cranes — hired from the appropriately named Biggee Drayage Company — hoisted the guns to the prepared platforms, pneumatic tires still attached.

Once mounted, the weapons were turned over to Battery F of the 216th Coast Artillery Regiment, a National Guard unit out of Redwing, Minnesota, under the command of Captain Harry F. Freeman. The captain may have been given four new guns to operate, but he had not been assigned any additional troops. Since his unit was already busy guarding the Golden Gate Bridge and the docks along the Embarcadero, manning the guns on Alcatraz was logistically awkward.

THE **ARMY** **RETURNS**

During the first part of 1942, defense of Alcatraz turned into a commuter affair with Freeman sending a daily detachment to the island to man the guns. Early each morning, soldiers were fed at the Presidio, driven to Fort Mason, transferred onto an army launch and ferried out to the prison. Lunch came out to the men on a noontime boat. Each night, the troops returned to their quarters in the Presidio; they had no searchlights for night firing, so Alcatraz's guns were manned only during daylight hours. To add to the confusion, a different detail of artillerymen usually made the trip to the Rock each day.

Freeman assigned one officer to provide on-site continuity between various army personnel and the penitentiary staff. A 2nd Lt. Louis Griffith, a dapper young officer who sported a matinee idol's slicked-back hair and pencil moustache, was delegated immediate command of the island battery.

The lieutenant had an enviable assignment. Not only did he receive quarters in the island apartments, he was allowed to bring his wife and young son to Alcatraz for visits. Since he resided near his battery, he was also spared trips back and forth to the Presidio.

The Griffiths were quickly absorbed into the fabric of Alcatraz family life. There was one noticeable deviation from the lieutenant's military appearance, however; in keeping with the prison's tight restrictions on weapons of any kind, the young officer wasn't allowed to wear his .45 caliber sidearm.

Lt. Griffith's lone military presence on the island was to be short-lived. Before long, a permanent garrison joined him. The army soon tired of providing daily ferry runs for the soldiers, so in the fall of 1942 a detachment from Battery D of the 259th Coast Artillery Regiment was assigned permanently to the island.

Instead of coming over from the mainland each day, the soldiers had their own barracks in the solarium atop B-C Building, directly under one of the 40mm guns. Lt. Griffith (who was apparently reassigned to the 259th), together with two sergeants and about 40 enlisted men of Battery D, now composed the first true artillery garrison on Alcatraz in more than 35 years.

LIFE *DURING* WARTIME

The 70 or so island families formed a tight-knit community, and correctional officers and their wives were leery of the new arrivals. With an average age of 19, the young artillerymen presented a dilemma: the soldiers were envied and admired by island teenagers, but some parents feared the boys might suffer from runaway cases of hormones. GIs were soon paying an unwarranted interest in the daughters of the guards.

Many Alcatraz fathers had no compunctions about letting the soldiers know where they stood on the matter of socializing with their daughters; sometimes to no avail. Even after the rules were carefully explained to them, some fraternizing appears to have continued between the soldiers and the girls. At least one marriage resulted from the Coast Artillery's presence on the Island.

Once the young soldiers understood the guidelines of family life on Alcatraz, they were quickly accepted into the Rock's daily domestic activities. The young men were granted full membership in the Officers Club (Correctional Officers, that is), given canteen privileges in the island's tiny grocery store, and invited to movie screenings, dances and parties in the guards' homes. The soldiers even named their jeep "Betsy Ann," to honor two Alcatraz girls.

Many correctional officer's had once served in the military, and a bond with the soldiers quickly formed. The boys became part of the Alcatraz family. Aside from the fact they never seemed to wear anything except their army uniforms, the artillerymen soon went unnoticed amid the daily routine of the island.

Until there was an alert.

Numerous air raid drills occurred during the early months of the war, and when an alert was declared the penitentiary's siren would start to wail. Simultaneously, the powerhouse whistle was sounded in short shrieks. Off-duty artillerymen immediately responded from solarium quarters in B-C Building. Soldiers atop the solarium had easier duty; they only had to run about 50 feet. Soldiers who manned the guns atop the cellhouse, however, had to sprint up the steep trail and two flights of stairs separating the parade ground from the cellhouse. At the front of the prison building, they next encountered the wooden security stairs and four more flights of steps. The soldiers were winded before they reached the guns.

ENEMIES AT THE GATE

There were others who noticed the lack of blackout discipline in the Bay Area, and intended to benefit by it. Though details were unknown until after the war, there was considerable danger from hit-and-run attacks by Japanese submarines, nine of which patrolled the West Coast following the Pearl Harbor attack. At the top-secret midget submarine base near Kure, Japan, submariners

memorized the details of five Pacific harbors; Pearl Harbor, Sydney, Singapore, Hong Kong and San Francisco. Within a year, the Japanese Navy hit three of the five targets.

In early 1942, a garbage scow hauling a load to the Farrallones rammed something large and metallic just below the surface, which cut a swath 80 feet long in the American ship. In 1946, a Japanese torpedo was discovered buried in mud by one of the bases of the Golden Gate Bridge.

Several merchant ships were torpedoed almost within sight of the bridge. After a week of skulking near the Farrallones, the long-range submarine I-15 surfaced on Christmas Eve, 1941, just outside the harbor entrance, and prepared the 4.7-inch deck gun to shell the city. The other eight I-boats were doing the same — the shells were to be a "Christmas present" from the Imperial Navy.

As the gun was loaded, an order from Tokyo was recieved that hastily cancelled the attack. Recently declassified radio intercepts, courtesy the National Security Agency, reveal that the reason was to avoid injury "to those Japanese living adjacent to military targets," such as cities.

Few, if any, Japanese-Americans would have felt honored. Gen. DeWitt's zealousness for coastal security would soon lead him into mass arrests of these recent citizens. They were removed to "relocation centers," ironically, far beyond the range of submarine guns.

Once at their posts, the men clapped on steel helmets, uncovered the 40mm and .50 caliber guns, turned on the height finders, plugged into their telephone-communications link with the Harbor Defense Command Post in San Francisco, traversed the gun barrels and began scanning the sky for approaching aircraft.

It was quite a show.

Correctional Officer Phil Bergen was one of the guards appointed to the position of Air Raid Warden. Whenever there was a blackout it was his duty to patrol the family compound of the island,

A ready room for the antiaircraft crew, located atop the Model Industries Building during World War II. Made of box lumber and tarpaper, it's typical of the state-of-emergency construction of the period.

making sure that no lights were visible, and prepare to evacuate the residents if necessary. If enemy bombers appeared, the families were to be evacuated to an air-raid shelter in the casemated basement of Building 64.

Bergen sometimes patrolled the cellblocks during air-raid alerts. He recalled convicts curled up on cell floors, trying to crawl under steel bunks and crying while sirens wailed and whistles sounded. There was no air-raid shelter for them. They were obliged to wait in the limited safety of their cells.

Throughout most of the penitentiary's history, the Bureau of Prisons secluded Alcatraz convicts from much news of the outside world. During the war they eased this rule. The blackboard that had announced the news of the Pearl Harbor attack remained at the entrance to the dining room. Each day the warden's secretary updated the board with blaring reports of the latest American victories in far-away places like Guadalcanal and Rabaul. News about U.S. setbacks, the cons believed, was conspicuously absent.

The convicts also found themselves involved in wartime industries. An antisubmarine net had been stretched across the Golden Gate, and the navy periodically brought the net's flotation buoys to the island for repair. Many of the more patriotic inmates were assigned to sandblasting, patch-welding and repainting the buoys. Other inmates produced cargo nets for use on naval ships while the tailor shop turned out military uniforms.

Thousands of troops poured into army bases around the bay, and the Alcatraz laundry handled tons of soiled military uniforms. Soldiers stationed near San Francisco bragged that Al Capone laundered

their shorts, oblivious that "Scarface" had been transferred from the Rock more than a year before Pearl Harbor was bombed.

The convicts were well aware of the soldiers' presence on the island, but they had no information on the troops' actual role. The prisoners could only see the antiaircraft guns atop the cellhouse and Model Shop and catch occasional glimpses of the helmeted crews, so the institution grapevine filled in with bits of misinformation.

One popular theory held the AA guns were dummy weapons meant to divert Japanese bombers from real military targets elsewhere on the bay. Jim Quillen, who had the dubious distinction of being the youngest con on the Rock, thought there was only one gun; the weapon atop the hospital wing was all he ever saw from his limited recreation yard view of the outside world. He also recalled an especially vicious rumor — if invasion came, guards would kill the inmates in their cells rather than let the Japanese set them free.

No one remembers ever hearing the antiaircraft guns being fired, either in alarm or for practice, giving fuel to the cons' "dummy gun" theory. It's quite likely they never were fired, and for the same reason that during the Civil War, 80 years earlier, the fort's commander had been told not to hold artillery practice: the army didn't want to alarm the citizenry. Instead, the Alcatraz troops were sent to the dunes of Fort Funston at the southern end of San Francisco for target practice.

There was no interchange allowed between convicts and soldiers. The GIs only saw the prisoners at a distance, working on the dock unloading cargo or milling about in the exercise yard beneath the cellhouse gun emplacement. A few shouted exchanges may have occurred, but none in the memory of any of the guard staff. Soldiers were granted one special privilege that many civilians would have paid dearly for — individually guided tours of the interior of the prison building, cellblocks, and industrial work shops.

For the soldiers, Alcatraz was good duty.

A *.50-CALIBER* ERROR

Men get bored waiting for an enemy who never comes. They do silly things out of boredom. Officer Phil Bergen recalled one story of that long wait: One afternoon, midway through the war, a young soldier was showing off for his friends on the crew of the cellhouse battery. Horsing around with the .50 caliber machine gun, he was demonstrating how he planned to knock down any Japanese fighters that dared fly over his position.

"*Ack-ack-ack-ack-ack!*" he said, as he swung the barrel to the south. "*Ack-ack-ack-ack-ack!*" as he swung the barrel to the north.

"*Ack-ack-ack-ack-ack!*" as he swung the barrel to the south again and pulled the trigger.

More details of antiaircraft gun emplacements, this one atop the apartment building. The ominous-looking mechanical device is a gun director, and a canvas-covered machine gun peeks out behind the artilleryman.

The Browning spat out a single round, making a much more realistic sound.

There followed a silence very profound, broken only by a familiar curse word and the gentle tinkling of a brass casing bouncing on concrete. Eyes focused on the young gunner. "Maybe no one heard that," he said wistfully. He quickly pocketed the expended cartridge and its steel-belt link. He proceeded to give the weapon the most thorough cleaning it had received since it left the factory.

According to Phil Bergen, that night the army declared a blackout. Someone had fired a bullet at the Presidio, and the Western Defense Command wasn't taking any chances there might not be a Zero fighter flying around with a single-shot machine gun.

Two days later, Warden Johnston received a phone call from the Presidio. The Military Police, following-up on the investigation of the mystery shot, had determined that it had come from a U.S. weapon, probably located on Alcatraz. The MPs requested permission to come to the island and ask some questions.

Amazingly, none of the prison staff had heard the shot. When the young artillerymen were asked by the MPs about any unauthorized firing of their weapons, the soldiers were shocked at the accusation. And you could have eaten lasagna out of the barrel of that machine gun on top of the cellhouse.

Word of the accident eventually leaked down to the prison's associate warden several days later. "What the hell," he thought, "No one was killed, were they?" And Warden Johnston — perhaps still smarting from Gen. DeWitt's meddling in blackout regulations — had no intention of turning in the GI.

Officially, the incident never occurred.

Years later, Bergen recalled an interesting fact that seems to have eluded the army investigators. The guard post known as Main Tower

was located only a few feet from the machine gun, and the tower had been manned at the time of the incident. The guard who pulled the duty that day had either been deaf, or intentionally decided not to say anything to his own supervisor or to the MPs.

Alcatraz took care of its own.

The artillerymen left long before V-J day. There was no reason to keep them on Alcatraz any longer. No Japanese bombers would be flying over San Francisco at this late date in the war, and the place for trained soldiers was in the planned invasion of Japan, not guarding federal penitentiaries.

In late 1944, the antiaircraft guns and equipment were lowered from the roofs of the cellhouse, apartment and industry buildings. The temporary stairway, ready rooms, magazines and gun mounts were torn down. The Bureau of Prisons, stinging from wartime shortages, requested the salvaged lumber from the gun emplacements for use in the penitentiary. Finally, the solarium atop B-C building was stripped of cots and lockers.

There was no trace that the Coast Artillery had manned a battery on Alcatraz Island for nearly three years, except in the memory of island residents.

The military last embarked on Alcatraz to quell a riot in May, 1946. Army and Marine units fired grenades through cellhouse windows and drilled holes through the roof to drop explosives into the prison. Tear gas billows around the cellblock in this view of the three-day incident, which left two guards and three convicts dead.

138   "No Good _for_ Nobody"

"NO GOOD *FOR* NOBODY"

12

Nineteen years after the Coast Artillery boys departed, the Bureau of Prisons finally gave up on Alcatraz. The official justification for closing the penitentiary was that soaring costs and decaying facilities made the island too expensive to operate.

The unspoken truth was the prison had outlived its usefulness. Opened in an era of bootleggers and gun-toting gangsters, Alcatraz had never been the deterrent to crime it had been prophesied to be. Formal orders to shut down the Rock came from Attorney General Robert Kennedy, despite rumblings of protest from FBI Director J. Edgar Hoover.

On March 21, 1963, the last 27 convicts marched handcuffed down the main corridor of the cellhouse, surrounded by a horde of invited newsmen and illuminated by a blaze of flashbulbs. The final prisoner to leave was Frank Weatherman, a baby-faced robber from Alaska, who got off a solid quote for the eager reporters: *"All of us are glad to get off. It's good for me and everyone. Alcatraz was never no good for nobody."*

As the convicts were removed, the debate began: what do we do with Alcatraz? The *San Francisco Examiner* sponsored a contest seeking inventive ideas for the crumbling prison, and suggestions poured in ranging from bird sanctuaries to gargantuan statues symbolizing peace throughout the Pacific basin.

In November 1969, a group of militant Native Americans calling themselves the "Indians of All Tribes" briefly halted the controversy when they occupied the island and announced plans to transform it into Thunderbird University.

Indian tenure lasted 19 months, their hopes for a Native American study center declining into anarchy and vandalism. The occupation started on a high note, but realities of living on Alcatraz soon became apparent. The occupiers desperately needed

Plans for possible future uses of Alcatraz, such as the American Indian University announced below, eventually went up in smoke as fires broke out during the occupation of 1969-1971.

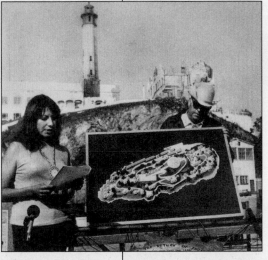

The dock area during the Indian occupation. Many buildings facing the water, including the powerhouse smokestack and water tower, had slogans added. Below, much of the original Civil War brickwork remains today, and is being restored.

everything from diapers to bottled water, and they opened Alcatraz to anyone bringing supplies. Swarms of curiosity seekers got onto the island, many of whom were more interested in partying and destruction than Native American ideals.

Soon, boatloads of copper pipe and wire, torn out of the island's utility systems, were being hauled to the mainland and sold as scrap to support the few occupiers toughing out the last, black months.

Federal officials eventually decided to step in and end the destruction of government property. The tragicomic takeover finally ended in June, 1971. U.S. Marshals arrested the last 15 occupiers, cited them for theft of United States property, and released them.

Once again the island was adrift in a sea of conflicting plans and arguments. Congress settled any debate with creation of the Golden Gate National Recreation Area in 1972. It included Alcatraz within the boundaries of the huge urban park, and National Park Service Rangers drew the duty of managing the Rock, but with a difference: for the first time the island would be opened to the public.

Park Service planners decided to satisfy people's curiosity about Alcatraz (and defuse its image as America's Devil's Island) by offering guided tours on a trial basis. They figured interest would level off after five years or so, and planning for Alcatraz could take place in an objective manner. The bureaucrats underestimated the lure of the long-forbidden Rock.

"No Good *for* Nobody"

Alcatraz opened in October, 1973, and during the next twelve months more people arrived on the island than during its entire preceding history. Tours sold out months in advance, and tickets became as sought-after as passes to a 49ers-Raiders game.

Interest has refused to go away, and has skyrocketed. By the year 2000, more than a million people a year were visiting the Rock.

The tourists may have come to see Al Capone's cell and query rangers as to the location of the gas chamber (sorry, no such facility on Alcatraz), but they also discovered a beautiful little island with stunning views and abundant natural life. And the Rock is honeycombed with history. Stark prison buildings stood alongside romantic, Spanish-styled ruins, and mysterious brick tunnels led to dead-end passages beneath rusting guard towers. Alcatraz came to be recognized as more than an abandoned penitentiary in the middle of San Francisco Bay. Its natural and cultural history spans centuries, and the public wanted to see more.

The National Park Service eventually developed a master plan for the preservation and interpretation of the island's long history. The main prison building would be retained, of course, telling the story of the Disciplinary Barracks and the federal penitentiary. Other portions would also be opened. Someday visitors would see the long-hidden rocky shores and tide pools dotting Alcatraz' perimeter, while the expansive parade ground would be landscaped for what was euphe-

The author leads a tour through the remains of the Citadel in 1974. The island continues to give up secrets — below is the breech of an 8-inch Columbiad cannon found on shore and believed to be the gun that burst open during an 1861 target practice.

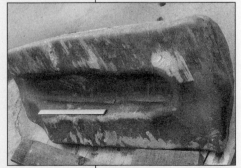

mistically titled "unstructured recreation" — Parks-speak for picnicking and enjoying spectacular views.

Various other historic buildings were recommended for preservation and adaptation to new uses, and portions of the old fortifications were to be uncovered and preserved. Plans were developed to restore the guardhouse to its 19th-century appearance, complete with drawbridge and flank howitzer cannon.

Natural life returned to Alcatraz following its opening as a National Park. Western gulls built hundreds of nests on the island's craggy slopes, and a small population of black-crowned night herons began raising noisy broods in trees spouting amid rubble on the parade ground. For the first time in more than a century, the island sounds like it did when surveyed by Lt. Warner in 1847. Plans for opening up additional areas on the Rock have to respect the birds' squatters' rights, though, and at present much of the island is closed for eight months of the year while the gulls and herons roost.

The wheels of government grind slow and they grind fine. At the time of this writing, the decades-old Alcatraz master plan is mostly just that — a plan. Visitors to the island still chiefly visit the main prison building, walk the switchback road up from the dock and, in non-bird season, follow a short trail along the southern shore. Other areas can only be visited on guided programs offered by rangers.

If all goes well, though, other phases of an "open island" concept will be completed in the mid-2000s. A perimeter trail leading along the edge of the island will be opened, followed by major clean-up of

"NO GOOD FOR NOBODY"

the former barracks, warehouses and industries buildings and their transformation to educational uses. In the interim, the story of the fortress and military prison will be interpreted primarily through guided tours, displays and models in the island's museum.

Most of Alcatraz's gun batteries, scarp walls and caponiers were buried during 19th-century remodeling projects and the excavation of the parade ground. Researchers tracing the contours and elevations of the fortifications theorize that many ruins are yet to be discovered.

The remains of all four of the original 1850s barbette batteries and many of the brick-lined emplacements of Col. Mendell's "Plan of 1870" are likely intact under tons of landfill. The foundations of Upper Prison may also remain just below the concrete pavement laid atop the parade ground in the 1920s. Massive archaeological studies and lengthy historic research will have to precede any actual excavation and restoration of these sites.

Much of Alcatraz' history lies just below the surface.

Today, the Rock remains a mystery.

Alcatraz today retains the profile it had in the early 1960s, without the addition of meditation pyramids, theme parks or gigantic statues. The National Park Service has politely and emphatically rejected all such plans.

ABOUT *THIS* BOOK

ABOUT THIS BOOK

I grew up in San Francisco in the 1950s and '60s. Alcatraz Island was a constant presence, but not one that I thought much about. The Rock was simply always there, in the middle of the bay, surrounded by equal parts barbed wire and mythology. My parents would dutifully point out the island to out-of-town visitors, who responded by taking blurry Kodak snapshots from Fishermen's Wharf or Telegraph Hill.

The only times I noticed Alcatraz came during Bay Cruise sightseeing journeys around the island. I'd watch for armed guards pacing their catwalks and hope to catch a glimpse of "gangsters" walking along the paths of the island. I saw plenty of guards. Never saw any convicts. But I was only ten, and got distracted by feeding the seagulls.

In the spring of 1962, Alcatraz suddenly sprang into my consciousness when three convicts managed to wriggle out of their cells and actually escape from the island. My fifth-grade classmates and I all anticipated what we'd do when Frank Lee Morris and the Anglin brothers turned up in the playground of Our Lady of Mercy Grammar School. I distinctly remember making machine-gun noises and declaring how I'd use judo to subdue the escapees and haul them to the FBI. Should any of the escapees actually have turned up at our school, they'd have had more to fear than a swarm of noisy, corduroy-clad kids — there was the wrath of the nuns, particularly the sister who bore an uncanny resemblance to Woodrow Wilson and who was a master of psychological warfare. The cons would have headed straight back to The Rock.

My fascination with Alcatraz's history began shortly after the federal penitentiary closed early in 1963. Television station KGO was given free run of the abandoned prison to make a documentary. Filmed in grainy black and white, the film's primary focus was on the forbidding prison that had been closed to the public for so long. It also showed extensive, haunting views of underground tunnels below the cellhouse and overgrown fortifications. One lingering view zoomed in on a bricked-up tunnel portal leading into a hillside,

Where it all began — this basement cell in the original Alcatraz guardhouse was home to 11 Army prisoners when the fortress opened in 1859. Today, because of its historic significance, it is a candidate for restoration.

DEDICATED TO
DORIS
MARTINI, MY
MOTHER, WHO
TAUGHT ME
CALIFORNIA
HISTORY;

TO ROBERT
MARTINI, MY
FATHER, WHO
TAUGHT ME
MILITARY
HISTORY;

TO ERWIN
"T"
THOMPSON,
WHO SHOWED
ME HOW THE
TWO HISTORIES
CAME
TOGETHER

while narrator Roger Grimsby somberly intoned, "To this day, no one knows what lies beyond this sealed passage." I was hooked.

I began my career with the National Park Service in 1972, spending two years at Fort Point National Historic Site under the roaring Golden Gate Bridge. This stint gave me the opportunity to learn about 19th-century military architecture and technology — knowledge that later became invaluable in researching Alcatraz.

In early 1974 I received my first position as a Park Ranger on Alcatraz, and set out to discover what truly lay beneath the crumbling penal architecture. The island is a layer cake of history, with the notorious subterranean rooms and mysterious tunnels that lead nowhere. I knew that Alcatraz had been a major harbor-defense fortress during its early years, but realized that almost no one had researched anything about The Rock other than Scarface Al Capone's incarceration and various escape attempts. My years at Fort Point gave me the skills needed to recognize traces of the old fortifications, though I was at a loss to explain how they once looked. I set out to learn about these little-understood ruins, and in the course encountered repeated frustration and occasional illumination.

A major frustration was a lack of original references. Journalists of the 19th century who had visited the island, and attempted to describe its works, had misused military terminology, confusing batteries with barbettes, guardhouses with casemates, and so on. Histories written after the establishment of the Federal Penitentiary were rife with unfounded lore — "dripping Spanish dungeons" — as well as mistakes referencing key historic dates. Much of my work was a search for accurate, first-person citations and original graphics of the island, what historians call primary sources.

Perhaps the most revealing insight was that for 87 years before it became a penitentiary, Alcatraz Island had been home to thousands of army soldiers, families, and military prisoners. It had been a place of stark contrasts — masonry fortifications and delicate gardens, formal balls and escapes, cellblocks and gun emplacements, incarceration and love making, deaths, births. It is that long-ago, forgotten Alcatraz that is the subject of this book.

Helping make the past come alive has called for the use of many photographs. The pictures in this book are from a wide variety of sources, not all of which had identical standards of print quality. The photos here were scanned into a computer and cleaned up. The retouching, however, was confined to damage on the original prints and negatives, such as scratches, fading, chemical burns and dust spots. The actual content of the pictures remains intact, and hopefully clearer. This edition includes additional images, and all pictures have been reprocessed.

Many people helped me in my research, especially those people who lived on Alcatraz, either in its cells or in its parlors. To these people I extend my thanks for submitting to interviews and sometimes thick-headed questions: Mr. Kenneth Mickelwaite, who donated both snapshots and childhood memories; Capt. Harry Freeman, who during World War II commanded the first soldiers on the Rock in many years; the late Phil Bergen, retired Captain of the Guard, USP Alcatraz, whose amazing recall of details about the prison and the lives of the island residents was of invaluable assistance; and two former convicts of Alcatraz who shared memories not generally spoken of — the late Walter Stack, San Francisco legend and runner extraordinaire, who told me of his terrifying stint as a teenager in the Disciplinary Barracks; and the late James Quillen, former convict, free man and father who spent his last years talking to at-risk youths about the mistakes of his own.

Other researchers into California's military history provided me with a wealth of leads and references: Herbert Hart, whose 1969 report "The U.S. Army on Alcatraz Island" is probably the first published research to rely on primary sources rather than rumor; Dr. Robert Chandler, whose extensive research on California during the Civil War yielded invaluable information on the role of Alcatraz's garrison as it maintained order in San Francisco by collaring Secessionists; and the late Col. Milton "Bud" Halsey, who guided me through arcane terminology and the maze-like command and rank structures of the 19th-century army.

John Arturo Martini, January 1991.

Many of my colleagues in the National Park Service have been especially helpful: Erwin Thompson, my mentor, who literally wrote "the book" on Alcatraz and allowed me to borrow freely from his landmark historic resource study "The Rock: A History of Alcatraz Island, 1847—1972"; Steve Haller, friend and ranger colleague, for his assistance in document and photo research; Jim Delgado, historian and workaholic who encouraged me and shared files from his book "Alcatraz Island: The Story Behind the Scenery"; the late Charlie Hawkins, Site Manager of Fort Point National Historic Site, who kicked my tail when I needed it; Gordon Chappell, Western Regional Historian, who kept me honest; Ed Bearss, Chief Historian for the National Park Service; and the late J. Jerry Rumburg, first Chief Ranger on Alcatraz, who let me begin my research.

I especially extend my thanks to my close friend and editor Burl Burlingame, a historian, artist, model maker, photographer, writer and journalist who makes me feel humble yet capable all at once.

Finally, I wish to acknowledge all the anonymous people who spent portions of their lives on Alcatraz, but whose identities are now lost to history.

Fairfax, California
February 2004

APPENDIX

A

COMMANDING
OFFICERS *AND*
COMMANDANTS
POSTED TO
ALCATRAZ
ISLAND,
1859 – 1916

Capt. Joseph Stewart	Dec. 1859 — May 1861
Maj. Henry S. Burton	May 1861 — May 1862
Capt. William A. Winder	May 1862 — Aug. 1864
Lt. Col. Charles O. Wood	Aug. 1864 — Oct. 1865
Capt. James M. Robertson	Oct. 1865 — July 1866
1st. Lt. John A. Darling	July 1866 — Nov. 1867
1st. Lt. John Fitzgerald	Nov. 1867 — Feb. 1868
Capt. James M. Robertson	Feb. 1868 — Dec. 1872
Maj. Charles H. Morgan	Dec. 1872 — Dec. 1875
Capt. John Egan	Dec. 1875 — Dec. 1877
Lt. Col. Albion P. Howe	Dec. 1877 — June 1879
Capt. Harry C. Cushing	June 1879 — Oct. 1879
Maj. La Rhett Livingston	Oct. 1879 — May 1880
Capt. Edward Field	May 1880 — July 1880
Capt. Arthur Harris	July 1880 — Nov. 1881
Maj. Royal T. Frank	Nov. 1881 — Dec. 1884
Maj. Alanson M. Randol	Dec. 1884 — Oct. 1886
Maj. John I. Rodgers	Oct. 1886 — May 1887
Maj. William L. Haskin	Nov. 1887 — Oct. 1888
Lt. Col. Chas. G. Bartlett	Oct. 1888 — April 1889
Lt. Col. Wm. M. Graham	April 1889 — Oct. 1889
Maj. William L. Haskin	Oct. 1889 — May 1890

Maj. Abram C. Wildrick	May 1890 — Nov. 1891
Lt. Col. Francis L. Guenther	Nov. 1891 — June 1896
Lt. Col. Wm. Sinclair	July 1896 — Oct. 1896
Capt. James Chester	Oct. 1896 — June 1897
Maj. David H. Kinzie	July 1897 — April 1898
Capt. Charles W. Hobbs	April 1898 — June 1898
Capt. Charles H. Dasher	June 1898 — Sept. 1898
Capt. George B. Baldwin	Sept. 1898 — Jan. 1899
Lt. Col. David H. Kinzie	Jan. 1899 — April 1899
Capt. Ammon Augur	April 1899 — May 1899
Maj. John M. Thompson	May 1899 — June 1899
Capt. John D. C. Hoskins	June 1899 — Sept. 1899
Capt. George T. Bartlett	Sept. 1899—April 1900
1st. Lt. Lyman M. Welch	April 1900 — May 1900
Maj. James O'Hara	May 1900 — July 1900
Capt. Henry C. Danes	June 1900 — July 1900
Capt. Benj. W. Atkinson	July 1900 — March 1901
Col. Sumner H. Lincoln	March 1901—April 1901
Capt. Charles B. Hardin	April 1901 — May 1901
Maj. George S. Young	May 1901 — Oct. 1901
Capt. Elon F. Willcox	Oct. 1901 — Nov. 1901
Lt. Col. Abner H. Merrill	Nov. 1901 — July 1902
Maj. Bernard A. Byrne	July 1902 — Feb. 1903
Maj. Cornelius Gardner	Feb. 1903 — March 1903
Maj. Alexis R. Paxton	March 1903 — Oct. 1905
Maj. George W. McIver	Oct. 1905 — Jan. 1906
Maj. Abner Pickering	Jan. 1906 — June 1907
Col. Reuben B. Turner	June 1907 — Nov. 1911
Col. Robert C. Van Vliet	Nov. 1911 — June 1913
Col. Charles M. Truitt	June 1913 — Sept. 1914
Capt. Charles R. Howland	Sept. 1914 — Aug. 1917
Capt. Samuel M. English	Aug. 1917 — Sept. 1917
Col. Joseph Garrard	Sept. 1917 —unk.

A mystery photo — according to official records, Company G of the 13th Infantry never went to Alcatraz. Yet, here they are.

In June, 1907, the official post designation was changed from "Alcatraz Island" to "Pacific Branch, U.S. Military Prison, Alcatraz Island," and the title "Commanding Officer" was changed to "Commandant."

APPENDIX

B

U.S. ARMY
UNITS
STATIONED ON
ALCATRAZ
ISLAND,
1859 – 1916

Regiment/Unit	Company/Battery	Years
Regulars		
1st U.S. Artillery	A, B, C, D, G, H, I, M	1881 — 1890
2nd U.S. Artillery	B, E, F, G, K, L	1865 — 1872
3rd U.S. Artillery	A, B, D, E, H, I, K, L, N and Band	1859 — 1864, 1896 —1900
4th U.S. Artillery	C, D, E, F, G, H, K, L	1872 — 1881
5th U.S. Artillery	A, B, C, E, H, I, K	1890 — 1896
Coast Artillery Corps	63, 64, 71	1901 — 1902
1st U.S. Infantry	C, E, and Band	1888 — 1889, 1897
4th U.S. Infantry	B, C, D	1905 — 1906
6th U.S. Infantry	G	1860
7th U.S. Infantry	H	1900 — 1901
9th U.S. Infantry	F, G, H, K	1862 — 1865
10th U.S. Infantry	M	1905
12th U.S. Infantry	C, E, F, G, H, M	1902 — 1905
18th U.S. Infantry	A, C	1901
22nd U.S. Infantry	A, E, F, G, H, K	1906 — 1907
24th U.S. Infantry	H	1899
U.S. Eng. Det.	A	1861
1st Dragoons	Recruits	1861
Medical Corps	Conv. Co. No. 2	1900 — 1901
U.S. Military Prison		
Guards	Companies 3 and 4	1907 — 1915
U.S. Disciplinary Barracks		
Guards	Companies 3 and 4	1915 — 1934
Disciplinary Bat., Pacific Branch		1914 — 1915
2nd Disciplinary Bat.	5th, 6th, 7th, 8th Co.	1915 — 1934
2nd Disciplinary Band		
Volunteers		
1st California Vol. Inf.		1862
2nd California Vol. Inf.	G	1861 — 1862
2nd California Vol. Cav.	F	1864
5th California Vol. Inf.	H, K	1862
6th California Vol. Inf.	A	1864 — 1865, 1898
8th California Vol. Inf.	E, G, H, M	1864 — 1865, 1898 — 1899

Smoothbores — Mounted

5	15-inch Rodmans, barbette, center-pintle
8	10-inch Rodmans, barbette, front-pintle
4	8-inch Rodmans, barbette, front-pintle
6	10-inch columbiads, barbette, front-pintle
40	8-inch columbiads, barbette, center-pintle
12	42-pounder guns, front pintle
17	24-pounder flank howitzers, casemated
2	12-pounder guns, field carriages

Smoothbores — Unmounted

4	15-inch Rodmans
12	10-inch Rodmans
2	24-pounder flank howitzers,

Rifled Guns — Mounted

3	200-pounder Parrott Rifles, center pintle
5	100-pounder Parrott Rifles, center pintle
1	100-pounder Parrott Rifles, front pintle
6	42-pounder James Rifles, front pintle

Mortars — Mounted

2	10-inch siege mortars

Totals Mounted: 109 guns, 2 mortars
Unmounted: 18 guns
Total Ordnance: 129 weapons

Eadweard Muybridge captioned this photo "1670 and 1870 on Alcatraz."

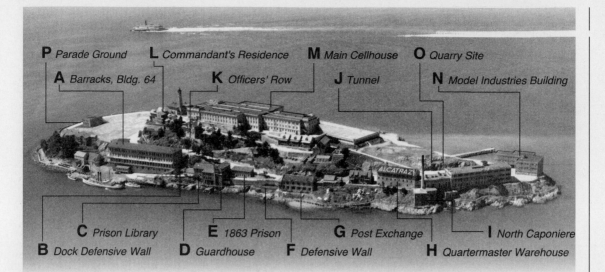

P **Parade Ground**   L **Commandant's Residence**   M **Main Cellhouse**   O **Quarry Site**

A **Barracks, Bldg. 64**   K **Officers' Row**   J **Tunnel**   N **Model Industries Building**

C **Prison Library**   E **1863 Prison**   G **Post Exchange**   I **North Caponiere**

B **Dock Defensive Wall**   D **Guardhouse**   F **Defensive Wall**   H **Quartermaster Warehouse**

APPENDIX

D

A WALKING TOUR OF FORTIFICATIONS AND MILITARY BUILDINGS STILL VISIBLE ON ALCATRAZ

The old Post Exchange, Area #G, was gutted by fire during the Indian occupation.

Many of the fortifications and army prison structures can be seen today on Alcatraz in limited form. Whenever possible in the text of this book, then-and-now pictures were used to illustrate these areas. Following is a "walker's guide" to some of the remaining features on Alcatraz, visible on either the self-guided tour or ranger-led walks around the island. The letter codes refer to the specific sites, and are arranged in the same order that an around-the-island hiker would discover these sites.

A   **Bomb Proof Barracks and Bldg. 64** — Immediately behind the dock are the remaining casemates and storerooms of the 1865 Bomb Proof Barracks, surmounted by the three-story, 1905 concrete-block barracks known as Bldg. 64. The old casemates now contain displays on the history of Alcatraz, theaters for video programs, storage space and island staff offices. A bookstore partly occupies the powder magazine remodeled by Col. Mendell as a mine casemate. The upper stories of Bldg. 64 underwent many modifications over the years, and the original barracks rooms and officers' quarters are now subdivided into a maze of apartments last occupied by the penitentiary guard staff and their families. *See pages 80 and 98.*

B   **Dock Defensive Wall** — In the 1850s, this 20-foot-tall brick scarp wall extended from the south end of the dock to the guardhouse, presenting a supposedly insurmountable obstacle to landing parties storming the wharf. The engineers demolished the southern end of the wall in 1865 and replaced it with the casemates of the Bomb-Proof Barracks. The wall was originally capped with a granite parapet, but most of the crest has been chopped down into a stair-stepped configuration. The stretch of wall between the casemates and the guardhouse is the location of the 1857 cave-in that resulted in the first two deaths on the Island. *See page 123.*

C   **Prison Library** — The roadway runs underneath this two-story brick structure, built against the exterior of the dock defensive wall about 1870 — the exact date is still something of a mystery to historians. In comparison to the fine brickwork of the defensive wall, the exterior of the library is very roughly built, mute testimony to the untrained labors of army convicts who erected it. It originally served as a combination library, read-

ing room and chapel for soldiers and prisoners, but over the decades it was remodeled for uses as a tailor shop, gymnasium, court-martial room, book-binder's shop, theater, ordnance storehouse and indoor target range for penitentiary guards. *See pages 70 and 123.*

D   **Guardhouse** — Constructed in 1857, the Guardhouse has been greatly modified over the years. The twin arches of the sallyport remain intact, but the drawbridge and oak doors are long removed. The Park Service recently cut away part of the roadway, revealing the dry moat in front of the sole remaining howitzer embrasure. Covered by the wooden floor of the library overhead is the lintel above the drawbridge, engraved with the legend ALCA-TRACES ISLAND 1857. In the howitzer rooms on the inland side of the sally port, is a 24-pounder howitzer on a replica carriage. Curved granite blocks in the floor of the bay side gunroom once held iron traverse rails for an additional pair of howitzers. Beneath this gunroom is the original dungeon where garrison prisoners were first incarcerated in 1859. The wooden cellblocks and brick library wing of Lower Prison eventually surrounded the original guardhouse, leaving its rectangu-

lar outline nearly unrecognizable. In the process of adapting the old gunrooms and basement dungeon for prison use, work crews widened most of the rifle slits into oversized window openings and tore out two of the howitzer embrasures. The flat roof of the guardhouse, originally designed for riflemen, is presently occupied by a 1918 Mission Revival-style concrete building that once housed a cobbler shop and schoolroom for army cons. *See pages 63 and 70.*

A Columbiad smoothbore, buried muzzle-first, served as a traffic bumper on the uphill turn in Area #E. It seems to have disappeared, probably during a war-inspired scrap drive.

The original wooden cellblocks in Area #E have been replaced by a Mission-Revival style building that once served as a residence for prison guards.

E **1862 Prison** — This small building bearing the sign "Electric Shop" stands on the site of the cellhouse constructed during the Civil War. The original wooden prison was demolished and rebuilt in more permanent brick five years later. Eventually, the two long wooden cellblocks of Lower Prison were built adjacent to the brick structure, cantilevered over the roadway on this side of the guardhouse. When Lower Prison complex was razed in the 1910s, most of the old 1867 prison was also torn down and yet another wooden building erected atop its remaining brick foundations. *See page 71.*

F **Defensive Wall** — Located across the road from the 1863 prison site is the only visible portion of defensive wall that extended from the guardhouse to the northern end of the island. The parapet, once several feet higher, provided protection for troops moving along the roadway. The mess hall for Lower Prison was located against the exterior scarp face, immediately below the road on the north side of the guardhouse. Most of this wall was buried during 1870s modernization of the batteries, but historians believe much of it remains intact under tons of rock fill and 20th-century structures. *See page 62.*

G **Post Exchange** — The Mission Revival walls are all that remain of the 1910 Post Exchange building. Built atop the old defensive wall, the upper floor held a canteen and barbershop, and the lower level a gymnasium with two bowling alleys. The Post Exchange was sometimes referred to by the army as the "Soldier's Clubhouse," and by the penitentiary staff as the "Social Hall" or "Officers' Club." It burned in 1970 during the Indian Occupation of the island. *See page 152.*

H **Quartermaster Warehouse and Powerhouse** — The road beyond the Post Exchange leads to site of North Battery and Battery Halleck, now covered by the four-story Quartermaster Warehouse (1921) and the Powerhouse complex (1912). North Battery was extensively rebuilt during the 1870s, and a series of earthen traverses and brick communication tunnels once spanned the road. Only one tunnel remains intact, but two bomb-proof storerooms in the west bank of the hillside are still visible. The Quartermaster Warehouse held stores of supplies, a

garage, and various workshops. The Powerhouse originally contained oil-fired boilers that heated the island's buildings and powered electric generators and pumps for fresh and salt water. Badly vandalized during the Indian Occupation and stripped of its valuable fittings, it was partly refurbished by the National Park Service in 1988. Diesel generators now provide electricity for the island.

I   **North Caponiere —** Located on the east side of the Powerhouse is the remaining portion of North Caponiere. Originally two stories high, its top-floor gunroom was removed during the 1870s modernization work on old North Battery. The lower room of the caponiere was retained for use as a traverse magazine for the never-completed earthwork batteries. The magazine still remains intact, its most recent use was as a storage tank for bunker oil. Although cleaned out by the Park Service several years ago, rainwater seeping through the caponiere roof has mixed with oil leaching from the saturated bricks to form a stagnant subterranean lake. Future plans call for cleaning the interior of the magazine and its impressive vaulted ceiling, possibly making this area accessible to visitors. *See pages 43 and 155.*

J   **Communication Tunnel —** Col. Mendell wanted to provide a safe passage for troops and supplies moving across the north end of the island. In 1873 he ordered convicts to excavate this 180-foot tunnel connecting two of the earthwork batteries. During the penitentiary era, the tunnel was used as a utility chase for water and steam pipes leading to the laundry building. Barred grates were put over both portals in 1934 to keep prisoners from using the tunnel as an escape route. The Bureau of Prisons totally obliterated the western entrance when the present Laundry was constructed in 1940. The original east portal remains open, and in 2000 the Park Service cut a doorway in the Laundry wall to reopen the passageway. The tunnel is now used to lead visitors across (and through) the island on guided walks.

K   **Officers' Row —** Brick foundations along the east side of the switchback road are all that remain of three Victorian-styled "Gothic Cottages" built for the fort's senior officers in the early 1880s. The first two structures — including the Commanding Officer's former residence — were torn down by the Bureau of Prisons in 1940. The last residence stood at the south end of the row near the lighthouse and was used by the penitentiary as the doctor's residence. It also burned in the fires of 1970. Across the road from officer's row is a brick retaining wall and a granite staircase. Constructed by Lt. McPherson in 1860, the stairs originally led to the Citadel. A massive iron ring set into the base of the wall likely served as a tie-off point for heavy loads being hauled up this section of roadway. *See page 84.*

L   **Commandant's Residence —** This imposing ruin was the 15-room commandant's home, built in 1921 on the site of the old post headquarters building. Erected to replace the aging Victorian located just down the road, unkind gossip at the time speculated that the commandant really just wanted a grander house for his daughter's debut into society. In 1934 the Bureau of Prisons logically redesignated the structure the Warden's Home, and it served as the residence of all four of the penitentiary's wardens. It burned in 1970. *See page 122.*

M   **Main Cellhouse —** The massive cellhouse, constructed between 1908 and 1912, sits atop the highest peak of the island. Its Greek Revival exterior has changed little over the years, and the original granite portals salvaged from the Citadel are still used as entrances to the structure. The interior cellblocks, however, were greatly modified by the Bureau of Prisons during their initial 1934 conversion work and a subsequent, PWA-funded modernization program in 1940-'41. Only Cellblock A retains its original Disciplinary Barracks appearance with flat steel bars, individually keyed cell doors, and drop-bar locking system. Below the

From the top, the Quartermaster Warehouse in Area #H, the interior of the North Caponiere in Area #I and the Communication Tunnel in Area #J.

Looking uphill towards Officer's Row in Area #K. The concrete slabs visible in the lower picture allowed easy access to water and steam pipes under the roadway.

At right is the Model Industries Building in Area #N.

cellhouse floors are the remaining portions of the Citadel — a labyrinth of storerooms, kitchens, privies, and brick-lined water cisterns. Upon completion of the new prison, the army converted several rooms here into solitary confinement cells ominously labeled "dungeons." On the north side of the cellhouse is the stockade, unchanged by the Bureau of Prisons except for the addition of cyclone fencing along the top of the wall. The stockade was built atop one of Colonel Mendell's 1870s earthwork batteries, and below the yard's walls are three arched brick portals, now sealed, that once functioned as communication tunnels through earthen traverses. In 1910, the army converted the tunnel on the east side of the stockade into a morgue, complete with autopsy table and three "cold storage" vaults, adding a tiny Mission-Revival building over the original brick portal. These tunnels, magazines, and the remains of the Citadel gave rise to oft-repeated tales of "Spanish Tunnels" believed to honeycomb the island. *See pages 19, 104, 107, 109 and 141.*

N   Model Industries Building —
This three-story concrete building, built in 1922, received its odd name because its shops served as a "model" of military rehabilitation, where vocational trades such as blacksmithing and furniture-making were taught to prisoners who, in turn, were paid a token amount for their labors. The Model Industries Building sits directly atop the last gun emplacement of North Battery and Bat-

tery Rosecrans, whose exterior brick scarp walls are still visible below the industrial addition. Park Service planners are looking at ways to structurally upgrade the building and possibly adapt its spacious workshop rooms to visitor uses.

O   Quarry Site — Directly west of the stockade is the rock quarry, now occupied by a two-story laundry building built in 1940-'41. This area was originally a small inlet known in the 1860s as Pirate's Cove. Prisoners gradually filled the cove with rock spoil cut away during subsequent remodeling work on

the batteries. In the 1920s and early '30s, "Quarry Dock" was located along the seawall at the foot of the slope where vessels loaded broken rock destined for other construction projects. *See pages 112 and 113.*

P   **Parade Ground** — This six-acre plateau was cut away by military prisoners between 1870 and 1876. In the course of their work, the convicts pushed excavated rock over the crests of the old batteries and buried the Blue Stone scarp walls built by Lts. Tower and Prime in the mid-1850s. After the Spanish-American War, the parade ground became the site of Upper Prison and its stockade. The area last served as the location of

various apartment houses and smaller residences for the Bureau of Prisons' guard staff. These structures were demolished before Alcatraz opened as a park, and mountains of rubble are all that remain of the apartment buildings where Coast Artillery soldiers manning antiaircraft batteries were quartered during World War II.

Looking up from the parade ground in Area #P. All that remains from the 1902 view is the convict-carved cut below the lighthouse.

Buried Resources — A great deal of material was brought to the Rock over the last fifteen decades, but very little was ever taken off. The engineers who continually built and rebuilt the island tended to layer each new generation of batteries and prison buildings directly atop its predecessor. Even when demolition work did occur, the unneeded materials tended to stay on the island. Granite copingstones removed from old parapet crests, for example, were used for retaining walls along roadways and in the foundations of officers' residences. Frequently, excess debris was tossed over the cliff faces. The keen-eyed researcher can still spot discarded cannon pintles laying exposed at low tide along the island's shores, along with a tangled mass of old barred doors, broken machinery and rusting pipes. Future archaeological surveys may reveal extensive buried resources such as fortification ruins, early prison foundations, discarded ordnance supplies, and the post dump — always a rich repository, ripe with historic information.

INDEX

A

Alcatraz, vessel 119
Angel Island 6, 11, 19-22, 29,
35, 37, 43-45, 73, 81, 83,
90, 129
Aquila, vessel 40
Army Engineers 20, 23-25, 38,
47, 62, 63, 66, 129
Atlanta Penitentiary 120, 123-
125
Ayala, Lt. Juan Manuel de 10,
11

B

Battery Halleck 38, 65, 68, 155
Battery Mansfield 38, 45, 55
Battery McClellan 38, 55, 58,
61, 66, 67
Battery McPherson 38,
Battery Prime 38, 67
Battery Rosecrans 38, 55, 156
Battery Stevens 38
Battery Tower 38, 55
B-C Building 129, 131, 132
Bear Flag Revolt 12, 13
Beechey, Capt. Frederick 11
Bender, George 91, 9 2
Benicia Arsenal 36, 37, 45,
Bergen, Officer Philip 133, 147
Berta, Charlie 128, 134
Biggee Drayage Company 129,
130
Bird Island 11
Blossom, HMS, vessel 11,
Bomb Proof Barracks 50, 53,
61, 81, 83, 92, 152, 153
Bradley and Rulofson 47, 48
Britain 9, 11,
Broncho 80
Building No. 64 93, 99, 115,
133, 152
Burnett, Henry 48
Burnett, Governor Peter 48

C

Cabrillo, Juan Rodriguez 9
Camanche, USS, vessel 40, 41
Canby, Gen. E. R. S. 80
Carson, Kit 12
Cassin, Michael 31
Coast Artillery 7, 130, 131, 15
Coast Guard 33
Coast Survey, U.S. 11
Columbiad cannon 22, 24, 27,
35, 38, 47-49, 141, 153
Confederates 7, 36, 37, 39, 40,
42, 44, 46, 47, 49, 51, 52

Correctional Officers 123, 132
Cralle, Col. G. Maury 116
Crook, Gen . George 81
Crowder, Gen. Enoch 100, 101
Cuba 23, 86
Cummings, Attorney General Homer 120, 121

D E

Daily Alta California, publication 73, 82
Davis, Jefferson 36
Dern, Secty of War George 121
DeWitt, Gen. John L. 128, 129, 133, 136
Dietz, Capt. William 83
Disciplinary Barracks 7, 33, 109, 110, 112, 113,
117-121, 123, 141, 147, 156
Earthquake of 1906 99
Elliot, Lt. George 38, 47, 48, 50
Elliott, William 118, 120, 124

F

Fages, Capt. Pedro 10
Farrallone Islands 56, 133
Fights 117, 119
Fillmore, President Millard 16
Fort Barry, California 92, 135
Fort Jay, New Jersey 121, 122
Fort Klamath, Oregon 80
Fort Leavenworth, Kansas 80, 95, 121,
Fort Mason, California 99, 116, 118, 130
Fort Pulaski, Georgia 61
Fort Sumter, South Carolina 39, 61
Fort Point, California 16, 17, 20, 23, 29, 35, 37, 43,
46, 48, 56, 73, 101, 146
Freeman, Capt. Harry 130, 131, 147
Fremont, Lt. John Charles 12, 13, 15
Fuller, Capt. A.M. 90

G

General Frank Coxe, vessel 119
General McPherson, vessel 74, 76, 81
Goat Island 6, 47
Gold Rush 13, 15
Golden Gate 7, 10, 11, 16, 19, 22-24, 30, 35, 41, 55,
59, 65, 73, 134
Golden Gate Bridge 130, 133, 146
Golden Gate National Recreation Area 140
Greathouse, Ridgely 40
Griffith, Lt. 130, 131

H I

Halleck, Gen. Henry 49
Harpending, Asbury 36, 40
Hayland, Matthew 51
Helios 56
Hoover, Director J. Edgar 120-122, 139
Hopi Indians 77, 81
Immigration, Bureau of 100, 101
Indian Affairs, Bureau of 77
Indian prisoners 80-81
Indian Scouts 80

J K

J. M. Chapman, vessel 39-42, 51
Jamestown, USS, vessel 74

Japan 127, 129, 133, 135, 137
Johnston, Col. Albert Sidney 36, 37, 39
Johnston, Warden James A. 128, 129, 136
Justice, Department of 7, 120-122
Ka-e-te-na, Chief 81
Kennedy, Attorney General Robert 139
Kingcome, Adm. John 46
Knights of the Golden Circle 36, 41

L

Leavenworth Penitentiary 120, 123
Lee, Gen. Robert E. 52
Leeds, Capt. 32
Lighthouse 15, 19, 22, 24, 27, 30-33, 53, 67, 89,
90, 97, 105, 114, 115, 129, 155, 157
Lighthouse Board 31, 32, 97
Lime Point 16, 17, 23, 29, 35, 43, 45, 73, 74
Lincoln, President Abraham 36, 42, 52
Lomahongyoma, Chief 77
Lower Prison 61, 69, 71, 90, 91, 96, 100, 104,
122, 154

M

MacArthur, Gen. Arthur 87
MacArthur, Lt. Douglas 116
Manifest Destiny 12
Mare Island 16, 20, 41, 45
Marin County 16, 35, 45, 65, 73, 92, 129, 135
McDowell, Gen. Irvin 47, 48
McNeill Island Penitentiary 123
McPherson, Lt. James Birdseye 28, 29, 35, 155
Mendell, Maj. George 62-67, 76, 83-85, 90, 98,
143, 152, 155, 156
Mexican-American War 13, 67
Mexico 6, 9, 12, 13, 16, 36, 39
Mickelwaite, Kenneth 118
Mission Revival Architecture 97, 154, 155
Miwok Indians 12
Model Industries Building 156
Modoc Indians 80-81
Monterey 9, 10
Muybridge, Eadweard 55-57, 61, 151

N

National Guard 99
National Park Service 140-142, 146, 153, 155,
156
Native-American Indian Occupation 139-140,
155
New Prison 97, 103-107, 114, 115
Ninth Corp Area 128
North Battery 20, 22, 24-27, 38, 43, 45, 49, 65,
68, 98, 155, 156
Numbered Prisoners 111, 112, 117

O P

Ohlone Indians 12
Ordnance Department 49, 62, 83, 86
Ortega, Sgt. Jose 9
Pacific, Department of 36, 37, 39, 46, 51, 81, 91,
95
Parade Ground 43, 48, 76, 90, 112, 114, 157
Parrott cannon 61, 63
Pass Boys 118, 121
Penitentiary 7, 3 3,
Pensacola, USS, vessel 74

A stereo image of the USS Camanche being assembled.

Pewter, Daniel 28
Philippines 78, 86, 109
Pico, Governor Pio 12
Pirate's Cove 26, 27, 67, 157
Plan of 1870 66, 67, 143
Point Blunt 44
Point Bonita 56
Point Reyes 56
Point San Jose 2, 29, 35, 43, 56, 59, 70, 74, 116
Portola, Capt. Gaspar de 9, 10,
Portsmouth, USS, vessel 13, 74
Post Exchange 152, 155
Presidio of San Francisco 12, 17, 24, 25, 52, 56, 70, 73, 116, 130, 131, 136
Prime, Lt. Frederick 20, 21, 23, 28, 77, 157
Prisons, Federal Bureau of 122, 123, 133, 139, 155, 156, 157

Q R

Quakers 11 4
Quarry 112, 113, 157
Quartermaster Department 90-92, 96
Quartermaster Warehouse 155
Quillen, Jim 135, 147
Raccoon Straits 45
Republic of the Pacific 36
Robertson, Capt. James 64
The Rock, publication 112
Rodman cannon 37, 49, 50, 53, 55, 57-59, 61, 63, 65, 66, 74, 85, 98, 127, 142, 153
Rubery, Alfred 41

S

Sacramento 25, 48,
San Carlos, vessel 10, 11
San Diego 9, 10,
San Francisco Chronicle, publication 73, 75, 91, 128

San Francisco Examiner, publication 139
Satellite, HMS, vessel 25
Sausalito 46
Secessionists 37, 39, 42, 53
Shafter, Gen. William 89, 90
Sham Battle 73-75
Shubrick, vessel 44
Sloluck 80
South Battery 20-22, 24-26, 38, 39, 42, 47, 76
Spain 9, 11, 12, 23, 86, 114, 146, 156
Spanish-American War 86, 157
Stack, Pvt. Walter 109, 112, 113, 117, 147
Stanford, Gov. Leland 57
Stanton, Secty of War Edwin 49
Stewart, Capt. Joseph 29, 35, 37, 51,
Stroud, Sgt. 110
Submarine torpedoes 83, 84, 86, 152
Sumner, Gen. Edwin V. 37, 39, 42, 51
Sutlej, HMS, vessel 46, 47

T

Telegraph Hill 45
Temple, Francis 12, 13
Three Gun Battery 24, 38
Throckmorton, Samuel 35, 43,
Topographical Engineers 6, 15,
Totten, Gen. Joseph 20, 23, 35
Tower, Lt. Zealous B. 20, 21, 23, 25, 28, 77, 98, 157
Treasury Department 22, 31, 56,
Turner, Maj. Reuben B. 96, 97, 101, 103

U V

Unger, Jacob 28
Upper Prison 90, 91, 93, 94, 97, 104, 115, 143, 157

W X Y Z

War Department 23, 31, 32, 42, 47-49, 55, 89, 90, 95, 97, 100, 101, 110, 112, 116, 121
Warner, Lt. William 6, 19
Washington, D.C. 20-24, 35, 37, 38, 40, 42, 48, 55, 62, 66, 83, 97, 129
Weatherman, Frank 139
West Battery 24, 38, 42
Western Defense Command 128, 136
White Island 11
Winder, Capt. William 45, 46, 48, 51, 52, 55
Wood Island 6
Workman, Julian 12, 13
Wright, Col. George 42, 46, 47
Yerba Buena 6, 11, 13, 22, 29, 35, 56, 84

BIBLIOGRAPHY

BOOKS

Bearss, Edward, "Fort Point," Historic Structures Report, U.S. Department of the Interior, National Park Service, 1973.

Harpending, Asbury, "The Great Diamond Hoax and Other Stirring Episodes in the Life of Asbury Harpending; An Epic of Early California," San Francisco: James H. Barry Co., 1913.

Eldredge, Zoeth S., "The Beginnings of San Francisco," San Francisco, 1912.

Hart, Herbert M., "Old Forts of the Far West," Seattle: Superior Publishing Co., 1965.

Hogg, Ian, "The History of Fortification," New York: St. Martin's Press, Inc. 1981.

Ripley, Warren, "Artillery and Ammunition of the Civil War," New York: Van Norstrand Reinhold Co, 1970.

Lewis, E.R., "Seacoast Fortifications of the United States," Washington D.C.: Smithsonian Press, 1970.

MacArthur, Douglas, "Reminiscences," New York etc.: McGraw Hill Co., 1964.

Thompson, Erwin, "The Rock: A History of Alcatraz Island, 1847 — 1972," Historic Resource Study, U.S. Department of the Interior, National Park Service, 1979.

PERIODICALS

Chandler, Robert J. "San Franciscans View the Civil War," *Salvo* (SF), Spring 1990, pp 6-11.

Hubbell, John T., "A Bright Particular, Star: James Birdseye McPherson," *Timeline,* (Ohio Historical Society), August-September 1988, pp 32-45.

Popular Mechanics, "Destroying Obsolete Naval Guns With Dynamite," March 1920, pp 418-19.

Strobridge, William F., "California Letters of Major General James McPherson, 1858-1860," *Ohio History,* Winter 1972, pp 38.

MANUSCRIPTS

Thompson, Erwin, "Fort Mason and the Earthquake of 1906," January 1990.

Chandler, Robert J., "Fort Alcatraz: Symbol of Federal Power in Civil War California," July 1981.

ARTICLES

The Rock, various issues: monthly periodical of the Pacific Branch United States Disciplinary Barracks, Alcatraz, California; July 1917 thru June 1918.

Daily Alta California — Misc. editions
San Francisco Examiner — Misc. editions
San Francisco Chronicle — Misc. editions
San Francisco Call-Bulletin — Misc. editions

INTERVIEWS

Bergen, Philip, San Francisco, August 1987
Berta, Charles, San Francisco, April 1987
Dudgeon, Esther & Arthur, Alcatraz Island, 1975
Freeman, Harry, Corte Madera, California, June 1990
Farenson, Dr. Gale, Alcatraz Island, 1976
Quillen, James, Alcatraz Island, July 1990
Stack, Walter, San Francisco, 1975 and 1990

MISCELLANEOUS

Hart, Herbert M., "The U.S. Army on Alcatraz Island," report for the City of San Francisco, 1968.

National Archives, Records Groups 77, 92, 94, 129 and 393.

U.S. Congress, *Records of the War of the Rebellion.*

Various unpublished records, Fort Point National Historic Site and Golden Gate National Recreation Area collections.

ILLUSTRATIONS

"Beginnings of San Francisco" by **Zoeth Eldridge** — 10 / **Bancroft Library, University of California, Berkeley** — 1, 2, 18, 26, 34, 37, 54, 56b, 57, 58t, 58b, 59t, 59b, 68, 74, 151, 159 / **Burl Burlingame AirChive** — 19, 62b, 67, 70b, 71b, 80b, 98b, 104b, 109, 112, 115, 122b, 123b, 133, 137, 140b, 144, 147, 153m, 153b, 154b, 156m, 157b / **California State Library** — 52-53 / **Fort Point National Historic Site** — 8 / **Golden Gate National Recreation Area** — 13, 29, 64-65, 66, 72t, 72b, 75t, 75b, 76, 78, 99, 100, 110-111, 113, 118b, 121, 122t, 126t, 126b, 128, 129, 130, 131, 134, 136, 139, 140t, 140b, 142, 143, 148, 153t, 156t / **John Arturo Martini** — 12, 43b, 56t, 63r, 155m, 155b, 156b / **Library of Congress** — 155t / **National Archives** — 7, 17, 28, 30, 33, 36, 60, 62t, 63 left, 69, 70t, 71t, 79, 80t, 84t, 85, 86, 87, 88, 89, 90, 91, 92, 93, 94-95, 96, 97, 98t, 101, 102, 104t, 105t, 105b, 106 left, 106-107t, 106-107b, 107b, 114, 123t, 152t, 153b, 154t, 157t / **Rex Norman, National Park Service** — 23 / **Private Collection** — 117, 120b / **Florence Markofer Collection, Sacramento Archives and Museum Collection Center** — 21, 22, 27, 42, 43t, 44-45, 47, 48 / **San Francisco Maritime National Historic Park** — 14, 40-41, 41 138 / **San Francisco Public Library** — 32, 108, 118-119t, 120t, 124-125 / **The Southwest Museum, Los Angeles, Photo #P.4028** — 77 / **U.S. Coast Guard** — 3, 24-25, 31

Turn-of-the-century illustrations by U.S. Army artist Henry Alexander Ogden show how service uniforms changed from heavy wool dress uniforms in the late 1880s, above, to more businesslike olive drab and khaki jersey uniforms by 1902, left. Often, the two styles intermingled as the army was in transition. Red trim on trouser stripes, shoulder tabs, jacket cuffs and insignia indicated that the branch of service was artillery.

A private of the 24th Infantry during the Spanish-American War, a military engineer during the Civil War, a medical orderly during World War I and an army prisoner during the Great Earthquake.

An artillery sergeant during the Civil War with one of the great Columbiad cannons mounted on a carved-granite pintle base. By 1866, Alcatraz bristled with 40 of these formidable 8-inch weapons, plus six 10-inch Columbiads.

The little steamer Princess *passes Alcatraz in this bucolic painting made just at the end of the Civil War. Just visible atop the island is the Citadel and the lighthouse. (Credit: Bancroft Library)*

Although there were only nine of them, the largest guns mounted on Alcatraz were the gigantic bottle-shaped 15-inch Rodman cannons. These were backed up by 20 10-inch Rodmans and four 8-inch Rodmans.

A 24-pound howitzer mounted on a front pintle was the weapon of choice for Alcatraz' casemated batteries. The short "shell" jacket for mounted artillery was also popular among garrisoned troops after the Civil War.

A medical orderly in dress uniform shows off the emerald-green trim of his profession, while army prisoners wear the brown canvas work uniform. The guard in khaki wears a blue infantry cord and an unusual blue Mills cartridge belt.